W9-CBS-218

There Is More

Previous books by Ralph Nault:

The Only Foundation
Be On The Alert! Lion Prowling
Out of Confusion
Led By The Spirit
Manna From Heaven
No Place to Lay My Head

There Is More

Discovering New Depths Of Spiritual Understanding

Ralph Nault

Published in the United States

There Is More: Discovering New Depths
Of Spiritual Understanding

Ralph Nault

Copyright © 2014 Ralph Nault
www.ralphnault.com

All rights reserved. Except for brief quotations in critical reviews or articles, no part of this publication may be reproduced, stored in a retrieval system, or transmitted in any form or by any means—electronic, mechanical, photocopying, recording, scanning, or other—without permission of the publisher.

Unless otherwise specified, Scripture taken from the New American Standard Bible Copyright © 1960, 1962, 1963, 1968, 1971, 1972, 1973, 1975, 1977 by The Lockman Foundation. Used by permission. www.Lockman.org

ISBN: 978-1507889626

Printed in the United States of America

Cover design: Susan Stone

Contents

Foreword

From the time he first shook my hand on a cold night in Boston in the late 1970s, Ralph Nault has impacted my life more than anyone else. I have never met anyone quite like this Northern Vermonter. He is the most spiritual person I know, and his insights infuse the pages of this book.

In the nearly four decades that I have known Ralph Nault, he has been to me at various times spiritual director, encourager, mentor, and friend. God has used Ralph to bring the transformative power of the Spirit into my life, and he has brought much peace, healing, and comfort to my family.

Forty-plus years ago the Lord called Ralph to bring people out of the darkness into the light. Responding to the call of Jesus to follow Him, Ralph and his wife, Pauline, have brought a drink of living water to anyone who is spiritually thirsty. Many people have experienced physical healing, emotional restoration, and freedom from bondage through their ministry.

From the get-go I often found myself wondering, *How does he do that*? Sitting across the table from me, he'd say, "I am as aware of God's presence right now as I am of you." How does he know God's presence like that?

How does he hear God like that? What's he got that the rest of us don't have?

How does an unpretentious former electrician have that kind of power to touch other's lives in such a profound way? The answer lies in Ralph's simple emphasis: *go to Jesus and be led by the Holy Spirit.*

In the evangelical environment where I grew up nobody talked about knowing God's presence or about how He was speaking to them. Ralph taught that it is possible to hear God and to know the leading of the Spirit. This is the key to receiving more from God. After watching and wondering for years, I gradually learned to discern the voice of the Holy Spirit for myself.

Now I can function as a spiritual person and use the spiritual gifts and fruits to bless others. I too have profound experiences of revelation from God. What a tremendous breakthrough to realize this *knowing* is possible for all of us, not just religious or spiritually elite. Because we are made in God's image, our human spirit is capable of direct communion with God.

As Ralph describes it, revelation from God can happen at any time or place—while reading the Bible, in a dream or a vision, even while talking or listening to someone. When divine revelation shows us truths, suddenly we see something we've never seen before. It's like being in a dark room when someone turns on the light—we are amazed at all the things we can see that we were blind to before.

That kind of seeing doesn't come from the reasoning processes of the natural mind—it comes only by the Spirit. It is a moment of revelation in our spirit, of seeing truth in the inner man. And when the Spirit touches us, it changes us, we become something more, we are no longer the same.

Several years ago the Lord told Ralph, now in his 80s, to write about the revelations that the Holy Spirit gave him. What a challenge to anchor on paper and in electronic bits his dynamic experiences—the comings and goings of a man of the Spirit. So, this book.

Spiritual mentoring and Christian education programs today sometimes neglect to teach us how to receive ongoing revelation from God and allow the Holy Spirit to guide our spiritual journey. The scripturally-grounded experiences described in these pages demonstrate the process of receiving more illumination from God.

This book vividly illustrates the many ways the Spirit brings us revelation from God today, including dreams, visions, and intuitive knowings. Numerous aspects of Christian life and experience are made more clear—from prophecy to decision-making, from natural reasoning to spiritual senses, from stumbling stones to faith anchor points—providing a guidebook to help people on their journey out of darkness into light.

When we *experience* God in a direct, personal encounter—as opposed to simply knowing *about* God—it transcends reason. Such an encounter, where we know because we *know*, is difficult to write about in a coherent, compelling way. Giving it his best shot, Ralph offers insights that impart to us the wisdom of a spiritual father.

Like St. Paul, Ralph comes not with "superiority of speech or of wisdom … but in demonstration of the Spirit and of power" (1 Corinthians 2:1,4). His revelatory experiences provide a rich resource for anyone seeking to deepen their relationship with God. In this book is *Life*, captured in plain, yet profound teachings that will touch your heart. It will clear up a lot of cloudy areas, reduce confusion, and enable you to move more into the light.

Jerry Doctor

Preface

Many years ago the Lord called me to bring people out of darkness into the light, as it says in Acts 26:18. I am aware that many people struggle with dark areas in their life. They get bogged down and they are searching for real meaning in their life. The Holy Spirit wanted me to write this book to help people on their spiritual journey from inner darkness into the light, into the truth.

The Holy Spirit was very clear about what I was to write about too. I was to write about the things the Holy Spirit has taught me—about being a spiritual person, using the spiritual gifts and fruit to bless God's people, and my experiences with divine revelation and healing.

To begin I must tell you that I do not know Greek or Hebrew. I am not a highly educated person as far as college or seminary education is concerned. I am not a great writer, capable of using large descriptive words or poetic prose.

I do not have a great theological background and I know very little about church politics. I cannot say I have much of a grasp of church history either. The Scripture that best describes my calling is 1 Corinthians 1:26-31:

> *For consider your calling, brethren, that there were not many wise according to the flesh, not many mighty, not many noble; but God has chosen the foolish things of the world to shame the wise, and God has chosen the weak things of the world to shame the things which are strong, and the base things of the world and the despised, God has chosen, the things that are not, that He may nullify the things that are, that no man may boast before God.*
>
> *But by His doing you are in Christ Jesus, who became to us wisdom from God, and righteousness and sanctification, and redemption, that, just as it is written, "Let him who boasts, boast in the Lord."*

The Holy Spirit has used the Bible, especially St. Paul's letters, as well as several other people and their writings to help me along the way. Some of these people were Watchman Nee, George McDonald, C. S. Lewis, and a man I knew and worked with for many years, Dr. Bruce Morgan. There were other dear friends, some of whom were Catholic priests and Protestant ministers, I have known and had the pleasure of working with down through the years.

Also our dear friends, Jerry and Judy Doctor (www.kairos-ministries.us), helped with editing, layout, and production. Without them this book would never have been finished.

Even though I listed the people who were such a blessing to me, it was the Holy Spirit who gave me the revelation. He was the teacher. They were the tools God used. Jesus Christ and the Holy Spirit receive all the credit for the changes in my life and for all the people this ministry has touched.

St. Paul was knocked off his horse and blinded: Jesus spoke to Him, and His whole life was changed. He left all the old things behind and followed Jesus. From that point He was led by the Holy Spirit and began teaching others to do the same.

I got knocked off my horse too. The "horse" I got knocked off was my marriage and my life that I had made such a mess of, to the point where I was considering taking my own life. My desperation brought me to my knees, and I cried out to God in a loud voice. He heard me and came and touched me in a very powerful way; I have never been the same. Thank God!

Seven years later, the Holy Spirit led me to my brother's house where I was prayed over for the baptism in the Holy Spirit. Within days, I had a great hunger for the Bible. I spent many hours reading it.

I was going to read the footnotes too; I thought they would help me to have a better understanding of the Bible. But the Holy Spirit told me no. I was not to read the commentaries either. I asked Him why, and He told me, "I do not want you getting filled up with what others think the Scriptures mean. You just read the Bible and I will give you revelation, teaching you what I want you to know."

This what I am writing about: the understanding He gave me. I will be using Scriptures from the *New American Standard Bible* and explaining, to the best of my ability, what the Holy Spirit showed me down through the years.

You may not agree with me; the Holy Spirit may have shown you something else. The Scriptures seem to have a way of saying different things to a lot of different people. But this is the way I understood them and applied them. And it worked very well for Pauline and me, and for the folks who God sent us out to share our lives with.

A Fool For God

I am a fool for God. Not only am I a fool for God, but for many people in the world I am insane. Why? One reason is that I hear voices, and the clincher is, I hear God's voice. I have heard God speak to me in an audible voice several times. Today, this is no longer necessary, because I know what He is saying to me in my mind and what He is writing in my heart, moment by moment.

I am a fool for God. I also have visions and dreams from God, guiding and directing my path down through the years. What's more, I also hear Satan's voice speaking to me. This makes me even more foolish.

I am a fool for God. Not only do I hear from Him, but I also try to do whatever He tells me. I am a fool because I lay hands on the sick for healing. I am a fool because I command demons to come out of people and stop tormenting them. I am a fool because God and the Scriptures have told me that I am a priest and a minister, and I believe I am!

Part One

Awakening

1

Growing Up

There are times when our language is very inadequate to express exactly what we are trying to say. We can listen very intently, trying to understand what someone is saying, but still totally miss it. It seems that the better we know a person, the more likely we are to understand what they are trying to say. Because of this, I want to give you a picture of my background so you might have a better understanding of what I am trying to say in this book.

I was born in Lyndonville, Vermont on October 5, 1930. My father, Frank Nault, worked for the Canadian Pacific Railroad in Lyndonville: he was a machinist in a large shop where they repaired steam locomotives and built railroad cars. He was a hard working man.

My dad traveled to work on a motorcycle, and he had suffered a bad accident and lost a leg just below the knee. At the time he was about to be married, but when he lost his leg, his girl friend changed her mind and decided not to marry him. It must have taken my dad a long time to recover from the loss of the leg and the girl he was going to marry, while at the same time learning to use his artificial leg.

Later my dad met another girl who he married. She bore him five children and died quite young from TB, when I was a year and a half old. At the time, the whole family was tested for TB; they found that my sister and I already had TB, but because it was in an early stage, we were able to be treated and recovered. To this day, when they x-ray my lungs, the scars are still on my lungs.

At the time of my mother's death, we were living in Lyndonville, not far from the railroad shops. My grandparents lived over in Barton, VT, on a small forty acre farm. When my mother died, we moved to Barton and lived with my grandparents on their farm.

As I remember, it was a good life. I enjoyed the farm and have so many wonderful memories from my younger years. Even though times were hard, we didn't seem to lack anything. I expect we were probably considered poor folks: we had patches on our clothes, holes in our shoes, went barefoot all summer; but we always seemed to have plenty of good food on the table.

Things were very different back then. Horses and wagons passed up and down the road in front of our house. Nobody seemed to be in too much of a hurry either. I remember so many times how we would sit on the front porch and watch the folks go by. We knew them all by name; some of the people would stop and pass the time of day with us.

We spent a lot of time on our porch, because my grandfather was blind from an accident with the forge. We had a blacksmith shop on the farm, and something had happened that caused him to lose one eye, then the other eye formed a cataract. Back then they couldn't do much for him.

My family was very loving; we had a lot of fun together. Sometimes we enjoyed listening to my grandfather's radio, even though it didn't always come in very clearly and only picked up a few stations.

One thing I clearly remember was the singing and music. My aunt lived with us, and she liked to play the piano. We often gathered around the piano and sang for an hour or two. I really enjoyed those hours. What a wonderful time it was!

Another one of my great delights was fishing, especially when my dad went with us. We lived a half mile from the village, up on hill overlooking a beautiful lake called Crystal lake: the lake was about two miles long, three quarters of a mile wide, and a hundred feet deep. It was great fishing back then.

In the evening we would go down to the lake and row out into the lake. Using night crawlers and suckers for bait, we'd catch two or three Lakers or Salmon, measuring twenty to twenty-four inches long. Those fish sure put up a good fight and were great eating!

I remember two unhappy times when I felt greatly distressed. The first happened when my sister was in the sanitarium for TB treatments. My father went to visit her and I went along with him, but when we got there, they would not allow me to go in so I had to wait in the car alone.

Looking out the car window at the large hospital building that day, I thought I'd never see my sister again: it felt like a big loss in my life. However a year or so later, she was able to come home, but that experience sure bothered me a lot at the time.

The second time was the day when all of my siblings went off to school, and I, being the youngest, was left at home. It hadn't bothered me when only my sisters went, but the year my brother, who was one year older than me, went with them, I was devastated.

From one of the windows on the western end of the house, I watched as they went down the road and disappeared out of sight. I was left all alone. Even though my grandparents were in the house, it didn't seem to make any difference: I felt alone! I was devastated, I cried. I don't think I got off the couch all day long. I just kept watching out the window for them to return. I think that was the longest day of my life. When I finally saw them come up over the hill, I can't explain what I felt.

The following days were not so bad; I got back to playing again, but that day had a big impact on my life.

As soon as I was old enough, I was sent off to Catholic education classes every Saturday morning and church every Sunday. I was not impressed with this. Since I was in school five days a week, I would rather be at home playing on Saturday. Besides, the Sunday service was in Latin, and I didn't have the foggiest idea what they were talking about.

Back then they didn't close the school on snow days. You bundled up with several layers of clothes, a wool hat to pull down over your ears to keep them from freezing, and a big scarf to cover your face and neck. We walked to school, and you got a mark if you were tardy.

Most of the Catholic kids went to the Catholic school, and the Protestants went to the public school. Even though I was Catholic, for some reason I was sent to the public school with the Protestant kids. This created a problem for me.

Because the Catholic school was halfway between the public school and home, I had to walk by the Catholic school. This was not a problem for me in the morning, because I was with my siblings, but in the afternoon I'd be all alone. I would get harassed every day as I walked home after school. This did not increase my love for the Catholic church or the Catholic kids either.

Many of the Catholic kids were French; we had a lot of French-speaking farmers who'd come down from Canada and most of them could not speak English. In our town, there always seemed to be a little animosity between the Catholics and Protestants. As soon as I was old enough, I just quit going to church. I believed in God and I prayed, but I just stopped going to church.

Regarding my school life, I enjoyed art and music. Math came very easy for me too; I didn't have any problem with it at all. I also liked to read, so I read a lot of books. But English grammar was another matter; I never really understood the rules and sentence structure—and I still don't. Because of my poor writing, I hated to be called up to write on the blackboard.

Because I could not remember things very well, I also had a difficult time with history and geography. My memory has been a big problem all of my life. As a result, I was not a good student. In addition, I never seemed to fit in well. I had a few friends, but they were kind of misfits, a lot like me. I also felt very self conscious; for instance at the school dances, I found it difficult to walk across the dance floor to the men's room.

I had a very low self esteem, so I was always trying to prove I was the best in whatever I did, and I always failed. I was a problem kid. In my sophomore year, I was asked if I wanted to quit school or get thrown out. I quit!

I do have some regrets concerning my school life. I wish I could have done better. Now I realize what part of the problem was: I had a short attention span.

Even today, I like to have several projects going at the same time. I write a while, play music a while, work on a puzzle for a few minutes, and then go and read a book for a while. Or I may take a walk, then go throw horseshoes for a while. I don't even try to stay with one thing very long.

I also had a difficult time visiting with folks for a long time. I always envied people who can carry on a conversation easily. I expect some people think I am anti-social because of my behavior and my preference for a quiet corner. I like people okay, but I seem unable to spend a long time talking about things that don't interest me.

Today the school system has improved the way they screen kids for learning difficulties, so the kids stand a better chance in school.

To add to my learning difficulties, I was color blind—in greens and reds. But I didn't know it until after I came out of the service and applied for a job at the airport in Chicago. I didn't get the job; if I couldn't recognize the colors, I might get run over by an airplane on the runway. In the early grades, colors are used in teaching, so my being color-blind had a big impact on my ability to learn too.

When I was about seventeen, I just left home and became a wanderer. I didn't really have any purpose or goal; I didn't know what I was doing or where I was going. I wandered from Vermont to the Midwest and on to Texas; I finally landed in Chicago, where my older sister lived.

At twenty-one, I got a draft call. I was given a choice of which branch of the service I wanted to serve in. I chose the Marines and ended up in the Marine Air Wing, spending one year in the States and one year in Korea. At the end of the Korean War, I was released from the Marine corps.

Those two years in the service were good for me; they brought some sense of structure and authority in my life, and that's what I needed. But I was still a very mixed-up person, without goal or purpose in my life.

2

A Deal With God

After the war I returned to Vermont, and there I met Pauline, my future wife. She was sixteen at the time, working as a waitress in the hotel in Barton. We started going out together and married two years later. I was twenty-five at the time, but I still didn't have any real goal for my life.

We had three children, two boys and a girl. Neither one of us was really equipped for marriage. The first four years were not so bad, but then it went down hill. We had a serious lack of communication, financial problems, and sexual problems. We wanted our marriage to work, but we could not find any real solutions to our problems.

At the end of seven years, we filed for separation and divorce. I made an appointment with a lawyer I knew: he drew up the papers and made the arrangements for the separation and divorce. He sent me a notice when it was time to go for the final hearing before the judge.

The evening before the hearing, I sat on my living room couch feeling very depressed. I looked back at my life and thought, *what a mess*. Then I looked forward: it all looked so bleak and empty. Here I was thirty-two years old, half of my life was gone, and it had amounted to nothing. It was at that moment, I saw a truth that changed my life.

All of my life, I had always blamed others for my failures. I blamed my wife for the failure of my marriage. I blamed God and the Church for failing me. I blamed my parents, I blamed my teachers for my failure in school, and I blamed my boss if I got fired. I always had someone to blame. But I was the failure—not my wife, not God, not my parents, not my teachers. I was the failure!

At that moment I took responsibility for my life and my mistakes. It may sound strange, but what a relief it was to finally stop blaming others. It was like I found a new freedom in my life.

Getting up from the couch, I went outside and walked up to the Catholic church I'd been a member of for many years. A young priest was walking outside the church and he saw I was very troubled. He asked if he could help me. I said, "No! I just want to go in the church by myself."

He said, "Fine, I will turn on a light for you. Stay as long as you want; no one will bother you."

I went into the church and walked up to the altar rail. Opening the gate, I went right up to the altar and lay down flat on the floor, on my face. I cried out to God, "If You are really there and for real, and if You will heal my marriage, straighten out my life, and give me purpose and direction, I will do whatever You ask!"

As I wept, the peace of God came down from above: it entered into my mind, and my mind was at peace for the first time in years; it entered into my heart and emotions. All the turmoil left, and I was filled with peace. The peace of God also moved through my physical body and healed my stomach that had been all messed up too.

Two hours later, I got up and walked out of the church. As I passed through the vestibule, a clear firm thought dropped right into my mind: "You are not to be separated under any conditions!"

The next morning when I got up, Pauline was gone; I never knew where she went that morning, until years later. She had gotten up very early. Troubled in her heart and mind, she had left the house and started walking up to the same church I'd gone to the night before, but she'd never made it to the church. As she was walking, she cried out to God for help; the Spirit of God fell on her, and she was delivered from an evil spirit that had troubled her for a long time.

We did not go to the judge or lawyers that day. We decided to remain married and try to go on with our relationship. About two weeks later, I called the lawyer and told him we'd decided to stay together and try to work it out. He said, "Praise God, I've been praying you would not go through with a divorce!"

In the next few years, our marriage improved day by day. We began to communicate and do many things together as a family, like fishing and camping.

Seven years later, as I was sitting in church one Sunday morning, suddenly I was aware that there had to be more to Christianity than just going to church for an hour every week. I know this was a revelation from God right within me. As I walked out of church, I told the Lord, "I am not coming into this church again, until I know what is missing."

For the next three months, I did not go near a church. Every morning as I started out to work, I would pray, "God, there has to be more to Christianity than what I have experienced, and I want it."

Around this time we began going to a prayer meeting at my brother's home in Newport Center. The second time we went, we were prayed over for the Holy Spirit to fill us. In the days to come, we were very aware that the Holy Spirit had brought new power and authority into our life and marriage, but I was totally surprised at what happened next.

About four weeks later, after we started going to this prayer meeting, we were driving home about ten-thirty one night. We lived about fifteen miles away and were half-way home, when suddenly an audible voice spoke to me and said: "I want you to start a gathering like that in your home!"

I looked over at Pauline; she was sitting there half-asleep. I looked in the back seat, thinking someone must have got in the car, but no one was there. Then I thought, *It must be my imagination.*

I drove another five minutes, then I heard the voice again. It said: "I want you to start a meeting like that in your home! Remember the commitment you made? Did you mean it?"

My mind went back seven years. I could see myself lying on

the floor of the church saying, "God, if You will heal my marriage and give me purpose and direction, I will do whatever You ask!"

I had never realized that God would speak to me and want me to do something. Then He spoke again, "I have done my part; I have healed your marriage, straightened out your life, and given you purpose and direction. Now I am asking you to open your home, so I can bless others."

Then He asked, "Did you mean what you said?"

I think my heart dropped right down to my shoes. I'd never expected God was going to take me up on my offer. I looked into my own heart, to see if I really meant what I had said to God; then I said, "Yes Lord, I meant what I said, but I can't do it—I don't know what to say or do!"

He answered: "I know you can't do it, but I can. You just open your home and do what I tell you. I will tell you what to do and what to say; I will lead you by My Spirit and I will not fail you!"

I said, "Well, okay God!" I opened my home, and He filled it with people; He touched many people there. He did not fail me.

God and I had a deal! He had fulfilled His part; now all I had to do was to fulfill mine.

3

The Call

After we had opened our home and started having a meeting every week, I thought that was about it, but we were in for a surprise. It was really just the beginning! We heard about a gospel concert that was going to be held just across the Canadian border, in a small Pentecostal church. Pauline and I both felt we were supposed to attend this concert, so we made plans to go.

The church was full; the pastor started with a prayer, and then he turned the meeting over to the gospel group. The music group was very good, and we were really enjoying the music. When they got to the third song, the Holy Spirit filled the church: everyone stood up, lifted up their hands, and began praising God.

I was standing up too, but suddenly I was not in the room anymore: I was standing in the midst of a violent storm; it was dark and raining, with thunder and lighting all around me. I was amazed—but I couldn't figure out where I was.

Then the lightning flashed again, and off to my left, I could see a low hill with a cross on top of it. I kept looking to see it again, and then the cross began to fill with light. It became brilliant like the sun, with spears of light going up into the sky, down into the earth, and off to both sides. The light came right at me, and it felt like it pierced right through me.

Then I realized what I was seeing. I was right in the middle of the stormy night, when Jesus Christ was crucified. I cried out, "My God, it is all for real!" and the reality of Jesus Christ, and Him crucified, entered into my heart and I began to weep. A moment later, I was back in the church standing with everyone else, and weeping.

I still don't fully understand what happened that night, but I know that somehow, for a few moments, I was taken back to the terrible storm when Jesus hung on the cross. It was real: I felt the rain and the wind; I saw the lighting and the cross. I will never forget it; whenever I think of it today, it is still as clear as the night it happened.

When the concert ended, the pastor closed with a prayer and said, "I know the Holy Spirit is still ministering to some of you, so don't hurry off. Allow God to do whatever He wants to do in you."

So I went over to the side of the church; there was a stool to kneel on and I knelt down on it. As soon as I did, the Holy Spirit fell on me, and God spoke to me. He said: "I have a ministry for you. Do you want it?" In a moment's time, He showed me what it would cost my family and me, if I accepted. Then He withdrew His presence, waiting for me to decide.

I could not make the decision! I wanted the ministry, but I felt I had nothing to offer anyone—my life was a mess! I did not know the Bible. I was not a religious person. I was not an educated person.

Suddenly the presence of God returned, and He said: "What have you decided?" I couldn't answer.

I finally said, "Lord, You know!"

He replied: "The ministry is yours!"

Here I was, a man with no abilities, no qualifications, nothing to offer anyone, and I have a ministry given to me by God. I didn't realize at the time that the Lord had given me everything I needed just an hour earlier, when the light had pierced my heart: when the light from the cross went into my heart I *knew* Jesus Christ was crucified and had died for my sins.

The Apostle Paul wrote in 1 Corinthians 2:1-2:

> *And when I came to you, brethren, I did not come with superiority of speech or of wisdom, proclaiming to you the testimony of God. For I determined to know nothing among you except Jesus Christ, and Him crucified.*

A few weeks later, there was going to be another gospel concert, this time at the high school auditorium in Derby, Vermont.

Again, we both felt we were to go. As the group sang its third song, the Spirit of God came down, and everyone stood up and started praising God. I stood up with everyone else, but suddenly I was not in the hall anymore: I found myself out in a desert.

It was hot and dry, with the wind blowing the sand; there was not a person as far as I could see, just desolation. Then about fifty feet away, a person appeared: it was a man dressed in a white robe, from the top of his head to his sandals. He just stood there looking at me for a few moments. Then He held out His hand to me and spoke, "Follow me!"

He turned around and started walking away. I knew instantly who it was, and that He was not going to turn around and ask me again. I hesitated only for a moment, and I started following Jesus.

Just as suddenly, I was back in the auditorium. I have no doubt that the person who said "follow Me" is the same One who spoke to James and John. I expect Jesus has spoken those words to many others down through the years.

God confirmed this call to ministry two more times. In the first one, the Holy Spirit told me to go to my Catholic church where I was a member and tell the priest what had happened to me. I was to ask for his blessing on the meetings we were starting in our home.

The following morning I stopped at the priest's home, thinking all I'd hear was that I was wrong or crazy. But what he said to me was, "God does these things sometimes. Go with my blessing!"

In the second one, the Holy Spirit directed us to go to the Pentecostal church in our town, not to join it, but just to visit. I'd never been there before. It was a nice service. At the end of the service, as the pastor was saying the closing prayer, he suddenly stopped and said, "The Holy Spirit has told me that I am to call out Ralph and Pauline Nault. We are to anoint them, pray over them, and send them forth in the power of the Holy Spirit to do the work God has called them to do!"

We went forward. All the people gathered around us, prayed over us, and sent us forth in the power of the Holy Spirit. The Holy Spirit came down and flowed through us—like a mighty river. I have never experienced such a powerful anointing in all these years of ministry. We were called by God to go out into the world and bring good news!

4

Has God Lost His Voice?

There are certain things we need to get settled in our heart and spirit, once and for all, regarding God's voice:

Can God speak today?

Is He able to speak to me in a way that I can understand?

Is He interested in communicating with me on a personal basis?

Can I as an individual come to know His voice in my heart and mind?

Very soon after I asked for prayer to receive the Holy Spirit, I experienced a great desire to read and know the Bible. I bought a Bible in English, one I could understand. I began by reading the Gospel of John. While reading it, I came upon some Scriptures that convinced me I could know His voice and that all Christians should come to know His voice:

> *"Truly, truly, I say to you, he who does not enter by the door into the fold of the sheep, but climbs up some other way, he is a thief and a robber. But he who enters by the door is a shepherd of the sheep. To him the doorkeeper opens, and the sheep hear his voice, and he calls his own sheep by name, and he leads them out.*
>
> *"When he puts forth all his own, he goes before them, and the sheep follow him because they know his voice. And a stranger they simply will not follow, but will flee from him, because they do not know the voice of strangers." (John 10:1-5)*
>
> *"My sheep hear My voice, and I know them, and they follow Me. "(John 10:27)*

Even though I'd had an experience with God seven years before, I never had a desire to read the Bible until after I was baptized in the Holy Spirit. I am sure the Lord spoke to me many times in those seven years, but I was never aware of it. I did not know His voice, and I was not aware that I could know His voice. I believe there are many Christian people like I was—they are not aware they can know God's voice.

It is very important that we should know His voice! Jesus said, "You will do all the things I have done and even more." He also said, "I only speak the things my Father tells me to speak, and I only do the things He tells me to do." How are we to say and do what He wants us to, if we don't know His voice?

We have an enemy who wants to keep us in darkness, both blind and deaf. God has not lost His voice; it is we who have lost our hearing. The Lord's desire is for everyone to hear Him and know His voice. The whole church suffers great loss, because there seem to be very few individuals who know His voice or are aware that they can.

Many times people have come to us and asked, "What is God saying to me?" At first I didn't know how to answer them, but now I tell them, "I know what God is saying to me, but I don't know what He is saying to you, because He has something different to say to each one of us."

However, some people do not want to hear what God is saying to them, so they ignore Him, like we do with our children or spouse. There are other people who do want to hear God, but they are uncertain whether it is God or themselves. They often ask, "Is this God or is this me?"

One reason for this confusion is because He speaks most often right through our own thought life. If we do not learn to weigh and test every thought as the Bible instructs us to, we are unable to recognize the thoughts that are coming from God.

There are two very important things involved in hearing God: 1) we must believe that God is speaking to us, and 2) our spiritual senses must be open to listen.

First, our faith is involved in hearing God's voice. We must believe that He speaks, and that He wants us to know His voice. There are many Scriptures that confirm God is still speaking. He is not silent in this day and age, but the Scriptures say the problem is with us: seeing we see not, and hearing we hear not.

Second, our spiritual senses must be open. The Lord speaks to us in a still, quiet way. He does not shout at us! When you learn to test all the thoughts that come into your mind, you will begin to recognize that some of those thoughts are coming straight from the enemy, Satan, and some of those thoughts are your own—things you want to do, places you want to go, plans for the future, and other things.

And some of the thoughts you receive every day come straight from God. They may be urging you to pray for someone or call someone. They may be directing you to go somewhere or do some special things. They may be just reminding you that He loves you and not to worry.

We can come to the place where we can recognize His voice no matter how He speaks to us. Have you ever had your mother or father call you on the phone? Did they have to tell you who they were? Didn't you recognize their voice right away? This is the way it should be with your Father in heaven.

> *Now we have received, not the spirit of the world, but the Spirit who is from God, that we might know the things freely given to us by God, which things we also speak, not in words taught by human wisdom, but in those taught by the Spirit, combining spiritual thoughts with spiritual words.*
>
> *But a natural man does not accept the things of the Spirit of God; for they are foolishness to him, and he cannot understand them, because they are spiritually appraised. But he who is spiritual appraises all things, yet he himself is appraised by no one. For who has known the mind of the Lord, that he should instruct Him? But we have the mind of Christ. (1 Corinthians 2:12-16)*

God wants to communicate with us in our everyday life, in little things and big things. He desires this more than we do. He has many things to say to us. We can learn to recognize when our Father speaks to us, whether through our mind, through Jesus, through the Holy Spirit, or through any other way He chooses to speak.

No, God has not lost His voice! It is we who are not listening! We are to be His spokesmen, if we can learn to listen.

5

The Healing Touch

Something else we need to get settled in our heart and spirit is the question about healing: is healing for today? Sickness is in the world, and it is going to touch us directly or indirectly. When that time comes, how are we going to deal with it? Some people deal with sickness much better than others, but the question is how am I going to deal with it, for my family and me?

Growing up as a Catholic I was told about miracles. I heard about all kinds of wonderful healings that had happened in the past. We even traveled to a couple of places in Canada where many miracles and healings had happened in the past, but I didn't know anyone who had received a miracle or anyone who talked about being healed by God today.

In my younger years, I'd go to the doctor or the drug store and get what help I could. I still go to the doctors and use medicine when I need it. I believe God gave us all these things, and we need to take advantage of them, but now, because of some wonderful Scriptures in the Bible, I have another source of healing: the healing touch.

As I mentioned before, I began to read the Bible when I was about forty years old. As I was reading Mark 16:15–18, the Holy Spirit nudged me to read it again:

> *And He said to them, "Go into all the world and preach the gospel to all creation. He who has believed and has been baptized shall be saved; but he who has disbelieved shall be condemned. And these signs will accompany those who have believed: in My name they will cast out demons, they will speak with new tongues; they will pick up serpents, and if they drink any deadly poison, it shall not hurt them; they will lay hands on the sick, and they will recover."*

I read these Scriptures over many times; I knew the Lord

wanted me to see something in them that I was missing. One day, I finally saw it: it was the part where it says, "They shall lay hands on the sick, and they shall recover."

I thought to myself, *I don't see any of this happening. We have several churches in our town, and I don't see anyone laying hands on anybody and healing them.* So I asked, "Lord, how come I don't see any of this happening?"

He answered me: "Nobody has faith enough to do it!"

I said, "Okay, Lord, I am going to try it and see what happens." At the time, I was an electrician, doing a lot of service work. Two weeks later, I got a call from an elderly woman. Her house had been struck by lighting and she needed help.

I went to her home and started work on repairing the wiring. The woman was sitting in a rocking chair, near where I was working. She started talking to me, telling me she was very sad, because she was going to have to leave her home soon. I asked her, "Why?"

She explained, "I had a woman staying with me, but she had to go into a nursing home because she was not well. I have a problem of blacking out, and the doctor tells me I can't live alone. I've tried to find another lady needing a place to live, but I can't find anyone. So I am going to have to leave my home."

The Scripture I had read came to mind: "They shall lay hands on the sick, and they shall recover." I thought to myself, *I have to try this.* Taking off my tool belt, I walked over to the woman and asked, "Do you believe in prayer?"

She said, "Why, yes, I believe in prayer."

"Then, do you mind if I pray for you?"

"Why, no," she said.

I knelt down by her chair, placed my hands on her, and asked the Lord to heal her, so she would not have to leave her home; it was just a very short prayer. She started to cry.

Feeling self-conscious, I quickly got up and went on with my work.

Two weeks later, I received another phone call from this lady.

She said, "I want to thank you for the prayer; I have not had another blackout. I went back to the doctor for a checkup, and he told me, 'Everything is okay, and you do not have to leave your home.'"

That did something for my faith! From that point on, I knew the laying on of hands works. I would suggest you try it and find out for yourself.

The question we have to ask our self is this: is there healing in the hands of believers?

I read in the Gospel of Mark about how Jesus laid His hands on sick people and prayed for them to get well:

> *And one of the synagogue officials named Jairus came up, and upon seeing Him, fell at His feet, and entreated Him earnestly, saying, "My little daughter is at the point of death; please come and lay Your hands on her, that she may get well and live." (Mark 5:22-23)*
>
> *And taking the blind man by the hand, He brought him out of the village; and after spitting on his eyes, and laying His hands upon him, He asked him, "Do you see anything?" And he looked up and said, "I see men, for I am seeing them like trees, walking about." Then again He laid His hands upon his eyes; and he looked intently and was restored, and began to see everything clearly. (Mark 8:23-25)*

Another question is: what is it that you have to believe? You must believe God still heals today. You must believe that He has put healing in the hands of the church, and in your hands!

Some people say that healing and miracles have ended: "That was just for back then; we don't need them anymore." But I know this is a lie from the enemy, to keep us from using the gifts God has given us. Miracles and healings are happening all around us if we have the eyes to see.

We need healing and miracles just as much today, and God has placed that power in His church and in His people. We must believe and act. Just look around you and see how many people need healing and miracles: the church is full of sick people who need healing. There is very little help for them, because we have only a few people who believe and have faith to act.

One week Pauline was very sick; she could hardly get to the bathroom. When Sunday came she told me she was going to try to go to church. She had all she could do to get dressed and get to the church, but an amazing thing happened that morning: the priest came out and said, "Before we have the service, we will have prayer and laying on of hands for the sick."

I was surprised; this very seldom happened in our church. The priest continued, "Anyone who is sick and wants to come forward, we will pray for you." As Pauline stood up to go forward, she was instantly healed: every symptom left her body.

But she still went forward and received the laying on of hands, because she wanted to encourage others to go for prayer. But no one else did. This was a large church, full of people. There had to be a number of sick people there that day, but not one person followed Pauline up for healing prayer. That is sad!

Jesus healed a lot of people, and one of the responsibilities of the church is to bring healing to the world.

> *Surely our griefs He Himself bore, And our sorrows He carried; Yet we ourselves esteemed Him stricken, Smitten of God, and afflicted. But He was pierced through for our transgressions, He was crushed for our iniquities; The chastening for our well-being fell upon Him, And by His scourging we are healed. (Isaiah 53:4-5)*

How are we going to bring healing to the world, when we don't do what the Bible says for ourselves? What are we to do when we are sick? The Scriptures tell us in James 5:14-15:

> *Is anyone among you sick? Let him call for the elders of the church, and let them pray over him, anointing him with oil in the name of the Lord; and the prayer offered in faith will restore the one who is sick, and the Lord will raise him up, and if he has committed sins, they will be forgiven him.*

Every gift of the Holy Spirit is very important; the church needs every one of them. Notice that most of the gifts are very involved with healing, especially the gift of healing and miracles.

Was Jesus interested in healing people? Read the Gospels; He was healing all the time. He even sent out His disciples to heal people and to cast out demons, as well as seventy others of His followers.

The church is called to bring healing and deliverance to oppressed people out in the world like Jesus did. Why isn't it happening? It is easy to look at our churches and say they are not doing it. This is not my point. You and I are the church: we are the ones who are supposed to be doing these things! The healing gifts are not just for Sunday morning prayer time; they are for seven days a week in our daily lives.

One day Pauline and I came home from ministry and found our son, his wife and little daughter waiting for us. As soon as we got into the house, they started telling us about their daughter: something had happened to her leg and she was unable to stand. They wanted us to pray for her.

I told them, "No, I want you to pray for her."

They said, "We don't know how." Since she was just a little tyke, I told them to set her up on the counter; they did.

I said, "Now lay your hands on her and ask the Lord to heal her."

They did. "What do we do now?" they asked.

"Put her down on the floor!" When her feet hit the floor, she took off running to go play. She was healed!

There is healing in prayer and the laying on of hands. I could write a whole book, story after story, of all the kinds of healings and miracles we have seen down through the years, because there are some Christians who believe enough to lay hands on the sick for healing. Praise God!

There is healing power for all of us, if we only have the boldness to lay our hands on the sick for healing.

If you have faith enough to get up and walk across the room and reach out to some sick person and lay your hand on them, you have all the faith you need. You can leave the rest up to God. All we have to do is lay on our hands and pray: God does the healing!

When we give some thought as to whether there is healing

in our hands or not, we have to acknowledge there is. If a child comes running to you, crying and hurting, you grab them up, hold them, touch them, and say a few words, and then put them down—and they run off to play again. Or when a friend has just lost a loved one, you go to them and take their hands in yours, hold them, express your love and concern, and something wonderful happens: healing and comfort touch a wounded heart. Because of these experiences, you must know that there is something very special in our hands, in our touch.

I was so blessed when in our church everyone started holding hands and saying the Lord's Prayer together. The human touch is very special. God has made it like this.

6

The Mystery of Faith

Now faith is the assurance [or substance] of things hoped for, the conviction [or evidence] of things not seen.—Hebrews 11:1

One of the meanings of *assurance* is substance, and that is the way I want to look at it right now. We have this mysterious substance in us called faith; it is a powerful substance, because it can move mountains.

The Bible tells us we have all been given a measure of faith. The question is: does this measure of faith work only in spiritual things or can it be used in natural things as well? Not every person professes belief in God, but because they do believe in other things, they are able to apply their faith in something.

Faith is mysterious. It is like our spirit: we can't see it, but we have it. I can see that some people are spiritual just by the way they act and speak. The same is true with faith; I can see some people using their faith just through their actions and speech.

Faith is very mysterious, because it seems to come and go. Sometimes we have all kinds of faith, and the next day we don't seem to have any. Faith can be stirred up or defeated by things around us or by spoken words.

One of the things I have noticed over the years is that some folks who have had some wonderful experiences with God are forever struggling with faith. One day they seem to have faith to move mountains, and the next day they are totally defeated. Other folks, not having some great experience with God, have a very strong faith that is very active in their everyday life.

Faith is like the air, because it is a substance that is invisible. You cannot see it with the eye, but you *know* it is there. You can feel the air when it is moving, because you feel there is a pressure against you; you can see the clouds moving and the trees and grass blowing, because the air is moving. You see the effect the air is having on things—so it is with faith. You can see the effects that faith has on people's circumstances.

One of the other mysterious things about faith is that, when it is active within us, we have peace in our mind and heart, even though we have not seen the results yet. But when our faith is not active, we seem to be lacking that special peace in our mind or heart.

As I began learning about faith, I realized I did not know very much about it. When I have asked other people about faith, they did not know a lot about it either. There seems to be a great lack of knowledge concerning this mysterious substance called faith. It seems the greater understanding we have of faith, the more effectively we can use it.

Recently I saw something new about faith: it can enter into us and then lie dormant for many years waiting for the right opportunity to rise up and transform our life.

I know when faith entered into my life. I was a little child and I was sent to the Catholic CD classes. They talked about God, Jesus Christ and the Holy Spirit. I believed it, and faith entered in. About twenty five years later, when my marriage and life was falling apart, that faith rose up in me and brought me to a wonderful experience with God and saved my life and marriage.

Many times we act and speak against our faith. There is something in us that tells us in a silent voice, *don't say that* or *don't do that*—this is our faith speaking to us—but we go right ahead and say or do it just the same.

> *But he who doubts is condemned if he eats, because his eating is not from faith; and whatever is not from faith is sin. (Romans 14:23)*

As the years went by, I became more aware of this strange substance in me called faith. I know it is one of the *most* important things in my walk with God. I need to learn to apply it, and keep it active in every aspect of my daily life. The Holy Spirit, using our faith, makes us aware moment by moment of what is good and what is evil, so that we are without excuse. I think of the verse in John 3:8:

"The wind blows where it wishes and you hear the sound of it, but do not know where it comes from and where it is going; so is everyone who is born of the Spirit."

Faith and the Holy Spirit are so much alike. Faith will lead us day by day, if we pay attention and learn to recognize the faith that in us and what it is saying to us. I have come to believe that faith can show us the way, more clearly than any other thing. My motto is: *If you don't have faith for it, don't do it!*

We often rely on our natural mind and reasoning instead of our faith. There is a war going on in us, between our faith and our thinking; instead of relying on our faith, we listen to our thinking.

We have seen many miracles, healings, deliverances and all kinds of manifestations of faith through the years. Nonetheless, I am amazed every time it happens, because my mind still has a problem with it. Jesus said there is great power in faith:

And He said to them, "Because of the littleness of your faith; for truly I say to you, if you have faith as a mustard seed, you shall say to this mountain, 'Move from here to there,' and it shall move; and nothing shall be impossible to you." (Matthew 17:20)

Our natural mind has a problem with this: it says, "That is not possible!" But faith says, "Yes, it is possible."

I look back at my life and see a lot of mountains behind me that I could not see my way over or around, but now they are in the past. I believe that faith will remove many more mountains before the Lord takes me home.

Can we place our faith in the wrong things? Yes! Some people have more faith in the church than they do in Jesus Christ. Others have more faith in the Bible than they do in Jesus Christ. Still others place their faith in some person or ritual or tradition.

We can place our faith in many things and get results. But it is important that from time to time we take a look at where we have placed our faith. Above all else, our faith should be anchored in the rock, Jesus Christ.

7

The Most Important Book

There have been many important books written down through the ages; you could spend a lifetime and never read them all. Many of these books are filled with man's wisdom and knowledge, but man's wisdom and knowledge are not enough. We need the wisdom and knowledge that comes from someone greater than ourselves: we need the wisdom and knowledge that comes from God.

In a wonderful book called the Bible, God has provided us with His wisdom and knowledge that has passed down through the ages. The Bible is the greatest and *most* wonderful book in the world. This book contains the most important message this world has ever received from God.

What is this important message? It is a message of salvation for mankind. But the Bible does not save us or give us eternal life; it tells us how to receive it.

Moses had to go to the Holy Mountain to see what God had written on tablets of stone. All we have to do is open the Bible and see what wonderful things God is saying to us in this age and generation. It is a message for all of us, not just a few special people.

We are still like the people who followed Moses: we want someone else to go to God and come back and tell us what God has to say to us.

A number of years ago, we were in a home group speaking about how God can speak to us in a very personal way through the Holy Spirit. After we finished, I was talking to a young man sitting next to me. I asked him, "Have you ever heard God speaking to you?

He said, "No! I don't want God speaking to me!"

I asked, "Why don't you want God speaking to you?"

His answer was, "I would probably die!" I was amazed; this is just what the Israelites said when God told them to come to the Holy Mountain.

I had read about Moses going up on the mountain and God writing the Ten Commandments in the tablets of stone, and how the people complained that God spoke only to Moses. So God told Moses to prepare the people and bring them to the Holy Mountain, and He would speak to all of them. But when the day came for them to go to the mountain, they would not go.

They told Moses, "You go, and come back and tell us what God wants us to do, and we will do it." The comment they came out with was, "Lest when God speaks to us we die" (Exodus 20:19).

As I was thinking about what this young man said, I realized this is just what happens when we begin to hear God in a personal way: old things begin to pass away, and new things begin to happen. It is called death and resurrection.

I have heard some refer to the Bible as a history book and it most certainly is, but it is so much more than that. I have heard others say the Bible is just a book of stories handed down from generation to generation, and we could learn some good things from it. Some have referred to it as the manufacture's handbook, while others say that it is just another book. What do *you* think?

To me the Bible is the inspired, anointed Word of God! It is the history of God dealing with the Israeli people, the Jews, and it is a teaching book that God can use mightily in our lives, if we allow Him to do that.

The words and actions of God in the past are written in the Bible. All we have to do is open it up and read it. Some say, "I can't understand it!" The truth is, if you have a fifth grade level of reading, you can understand most of the Bible.

There are some things in the Bible that are hard to understand, but pray and ask the Holy Spirit to open it up to you, for the Holy Spirit is the interpreter of the Bible. You can study it all your life from the natural mind, but never understand the message that is there. That message is very simple. Jesus spoke to the Scribes and Pharisees and said:

> *"You search the Scriptures, because you think that in them you have eternal life; and it is these that bear witness of Me; and you are unwilling to come to Me, that you may have life". (John 5:39-40)*

The message of the Bible is a very simple one, but very profound: if you want life, go to Jesus!

The Bible is a fountain of wisdom. It is filled with the knowledge of God and the Holy Spirit. It is like a mountain filled with precious stones and jewels, just waiting to be found by anyone who wants to search for them. You can read the words over and over, but until the heart is right, the truths remain hidden: seeing, you see not.

The Bible is filled with hidden things in both the Old and New Testaments, but you must search for them, if you want to find them. I don't think there is any other book like it in the world. This book bears witness to Jesus Christ, the Holy Spirit, and the truth.

The Bible is amazing in another way. You can study it all your life, become a great scholar and theologian, memorizing much of it, and yet never respond to its message or receive Jesus Christ as your personal savior.

Millions of people have received strength, comfort, and healing from the words written in this book. When my father was slowly dying of lung disease, he could not lie down, because his lungs would fill with liquid. So he had to sit upright, leaning on his elbows at the kitchen table. He could not sleep for days on end because he was afraid he would drown.

He would ask my stepmother to call me to come and say some of those "words" over him. I would go to him and open my Bible and just start reading. In a very few minutes, he would be sound asleep; he would sleep for hours and wake up feeling much better. This happened every time he was distressed and needed comfort.

There is great power and comfort in God's word in the Bible.

There have been times when Pauline and I were ministering to someone and the Holy Spirit would say, "Read this." We would read it, and the person would be set free of whatever was tormenting them.

Never forget! God has inspired the people who wrote this book, and God has anointed this wonderful book. This book has been instrumental in changing my life and the lives of many others. I expect it has had some effect on your life that you are not even aware of.

Most people believe in good and evil, and many believe there is a God. Some believe in Satan and even worship him. The knowledge in this book helps us to recognize the difference between good and evil, between God and Satan. Without this knowledge, we are unable to see the difference. You may argue with me and say, "We can tell the difference between good and evil without God's help!"

No! We cannot! Some of the things that we think are good are really evil. Some of the things we think are evil are really good. Only a spiritual man can discern these things properly; the natural mind does not even have the ability to do this.

The Bible is also a wonderful book about theology and psychology: it gives us both a knowledge of God *and* a knowledge of man. It seems that the more I know and understand God, the more I know and understand myself. Isn't that wonderful? As I see God more clearly, I see and understand who and what I am.

A number of times as people were discussing some subject, someone would say, "The Bible says this or that about the subject." After I read the Bible, I found it does not say the same things that some people seem to think it does.

I encourage you to read the Bible so you will know what it says about many different subjects. We take it for granted, because a person is a pastor, priest or Bible teacher, that everything they tell us is biblically correct. This is not true. Some of what they tell you may be what they have been taught by others who might not have studied the Bible at all.

The Bible tells us we are responsible to weigh and test everything properly; if we do not, we are going to be misled by well-intentioned people, or sometimes on purpose.

Something wonderful happens when we read this book with an open mind and heart, and listen to others reading it too. The words enter into our heart and become a part of us. When the Word enters in freely, faith happens, and we begin to believe in miracles and a miracle-working God.

I like to think of the Bible as the Holy Mountain that we can go to and have God write new things into our mind, heart and spirit.

Do you believe the Bible?

Is it from God?

Can it be trusted?

Start digging into your Holy Mountain, look into your heart and mind, and see what God is writing there day by day.

The Bible can be approached in several ways; it is important to realize this. We can have others read and tell us what it means. We can study it, one word, one sentence, one paragraph at a time, like a theologian would with the Greek and Hebrew meaning of every word. We can just read it just like we would any other book.

Whichever approach you take, you are going to understand it differently. If someone else is reading and explaining it to you, you are going to be receiving their understanding of it. They might be right; they might be wrong. They would be telling you what it means to them.

If you read it as the theologian or the student using the Greek and Hebrew, which takes a lot of intellect and learning to be able to do, you may end up with a lot of other people's thoughts and ideas.

I remember an elderly priest who I was talking with about the Bible many years ago. I was surprised to hear him say that I knew the Bible much better than he did. He explained, "I've studied commentaries and books other people had written about the

Bible, but I never studied the Bible itself."

I would encourage you to read the Bible for yourself and see what it has to say to you. Don't worry about interpreting it properly; just read it like you would any other book. The Holy Spirit will show you what He wants you to see, hear and understand.

I have come to believe that, to understand the Scriptures properly, we cannot rely on the natural reasoning of man. We must rely on the Holy Spirit to give us proper understanding.

8

My Teachers

In order to be taught we must be teachable and have a desire to learn. The Bible tells us that we can be stubborn, bullheaded, and stiff-necked; if this is our condition, I doubt we are very teachable.

There are two important levels where we need to be teachable: 1) the mind and reasoning of the natural mind, and 2) the spiritual level. We can be teachable at one level and not the other. The mind and reasoning of the natural man can learn a tremendous amount of knowledge that will be of great benefit to living and functioning in this world. Yet, we can have great knowledge at the natural level, but have no knowledge at the spiritual level.

For thirty two years of my life I was somewhat teachable at the natural level but not open at all to the spiritual level. I thank God that He opened my eyes to my sad condition many years ago, before I had a personal walk with Jesus and the Holy Spirit.

I was sitting in church one Sunday morning when, about halfway through the service, I had a wonderful experience: I suddenly saw there had to be a lot more to Christianity than what I had previously experienced. It touched me very deeply. Something rose up from the depth of my being and I said to God, "Lord, there is more to Christianity than going to church once a week, giving a little money to the church, and saying my prayers every day. There is a lot more and I want it!"

I share this experience because what happened was not something natural. It had nothing to do with my natural mind or emotions; it was a spiritual moment of revelation in my spirit. It was a moment of seeing a new truth in the inner man.

My spirit had seen a new truth, and it wanted more. As a result, I could no longer settle for so little. All my life I had settled for a very shallow, outward kind of Christianity, with no depth to it. This was not the fault of the church. At that time of my life, I was not even seeking a close walk with God; I wasn't interested in knowing the Holy Spirit or being a servant of God.

When divine revelation shows us truths, it is like we are in a dark room and someone turns on the light, and we look around in amazement thinking, *I never knew all these wonderful things were in this room. I was blind and now I see.*

Revelation can happen at any time or place. It can come in a dream[1] or a vision. You might be reading the Bible or some other material. You may be talking or listening to someone, and all of a sudden it happens—you see something you have never seen before. The best way I can describe spiritual revelation is to say it is like spontaneous combustion inside me; suddenly I see so much at once that it would take a book to put it all in.

Before this happened, I was like many others in regard to my relationship with God. If anyone would ask me about my relationship with God, I'd say something like this: "I believe in God and Jesus. I go to church; I support the church and pray every day. I acknowledge God and the church. What more can God expect of me?"

As children growing up, we had many teachers: our parents were our first teachers, then we had several different teachers in our school and in the church. All these teachers taught us many things that helped us to function in our daily lives and in our relationships with one another. Some of our teachers taught us purely from natural reasoning; others taught us spiritual things. I think for most of us it was a combination of the two.

Some people function better in life than others do; perhaps they were better students, put more effort into learning, or might have had better teachers or parents. Not all teachers are good teachers and not all parents are good parents.

---

1 For more on dreams from a Christian perspective, see books by Gerald & Judith Doctor: *Christian Dreamwork: 33 Ways To Discover Divine Treasure In Dreams* (2014); and *Dream Treasure: Learning the Language of Heaven* (2011).

Because we are body, soul, and spirit, we need to learn to function well at all three levels: we need to know enough about our body to take good care of it; our mind and emotions need control and balance; our spirit needs to be active and in touch with God and the world around us.

If a good foundation is laid, a building is sound, but if a building has no foundation or if the foundation is not solid, the building will continually have problems. So it is with our spiritual life. If we do not have a good foundation, we will constantly have problems in our spiritual life.

We have all had many teachers; each teacher was different and taught in different ways. I remember my dad teaching me so many things: he was a machinist, a tool maker, a carpenter and plumber, a black smith and a mechanic. I learned so many things from him just by watching him do the things he did. It wasn't that he was trying to teach me all these things—I simply learned by following him around.

This was rather strange, because in school they were trying to teach me, but I didn't learn very well. Now I realize as I followed my father around, I was a good student: I learned a lot just watching him and asking a question now and then. With this kind of learning, you do not have tests, nor do you get a diploma.

I had another teacher on Saturday mornings down at the Catholic school. There I learned some things about God and the church: how to behave in church, the prayers to say, and some rituals, traditions, and rules. I must say that at the time I didn't think it was blessing, but now I know it was. Because of this teaching, faith in God entered into my heart, and at the same time I received some much needed structure in my life.

A few years later, another teacher entered my life: this one was called the Marine Corp. This teacher was also a blessing, because it taught me discipline and order in my life. At that time of my life, I really needed it.

I would have to say my next teacher was circumstances and situations that happened in my daily life. Pauline and I were married, but we went through several years of very difficult things that brought us to the place where, with all our heart, mind and strength, we reached out to God and He was there for us.

The next seven years we learned how to function better with one another. I am not sure who the teacher was, but I expect it was Jesus and the Holy Spirit, even though I was not aware of their presence at that time.

Then I encountered another teacher who is spoken of in John 14:26:

> *"But the Helper, the Holy Spirit, whom the Father will send in My name, He will teach you all things, and bring to your remembrance all that I said to you."*

I have found that the Holy Spirit teaches us in many ways: He brings us revelation through dreams, visions, the prophetic word, and the Bible. But He also teaches us through our hard times, our friends and enemies—and even a mule speaking.

Before we started doing the work God called us to do, the Holy Spirit gave me a very important divine revelation: I was taken right into a vision, into a violent storm, where I saw the cross Jesus was nailed to. The cross filled with radiant light that pierced the darkness and came right into my heart. I spontaneously blurted out, "God, it's all for real!" and the reality of Christ dying on that cross entered my heart.

From the time I was a child, I had a knowledge of God the Father and Jesus, but it was all in my head, not my heart. During this vision of the cross, this knowledge entered my heart and has always remained there. (I shared this vision in detail in Chapter 3: *The Call*)

Now I have a new teacher who is interested in teaching me things through revelation, directly into my heart. Sometimes He gives me visions, other times He just leads me to a Scripture because there is something there He wants me to see. At first I don't know what it is, so I'll read it over and over, knowing there is something I need to see. I am searching for something—and I know it.

Sometimes it takes me a week or two, then suddenly I'd see it. It leaps right off the page, right into my heart and spirit. Revelation has happened, and I see a little more clearly. The more clearly I see, the freer I am. I can't begin to tell you how many times this has happened to me, and how blessed I have been because of it.

Another thing, seldom does the Lord give me the answer to anything; more often He gives me a question and wants me to search for the answer. Whenever the Lord asks me a question, my spirit gets excited: I know the Lord has got a new revelation to show me.

I know I am a called to be a teacher, too. I don't teach theology, rituals, traditions or the law, but I am to teach people how to hear God as He speaks to them and how to be led and taught by the Holy Spirit.

If you read all of the Apostle Paul‘s letters in the New Testament, you will find that this is what he was trying to do: teach you and me. He was trying to teach the church how to hear God and to be led by the Holy Spirit. However, the interesting thing is that, if you are not on a spiritual quest, you will not be able to see the things hidden there in Paul's letters: seeing, we see not!

There are many teachers in the body of Christ. Many of them are very good teachers, but not one of them can take the place of the Holy Spirit as a teacher in your life. Every one of you who reads this message still has areas of your life where you need to know truth. There are places where you lack knowledge, but only the Holy Spirit can give you the knowledge you lack, the knowledge that will set you free.

The Holy Spirit knows you. He knows everything there is to know about you; there is nothing hidden from His sight. He can teach you things about yourself that no one else can. He can show you things about yourself that you could never receive from anyone else. He can teach you things that no one else could ever teach you.

He was the One who was telling Jesus what to say and what to do. He was the One who was working directly between the

Father and Jesus. He is the One who works directly between the Father and us. One of the primary works of the Holy Spirit is to teach us; what a wonderful teacher He is!

There is a time in our life when the church is our teacher, but there comes the time when the Holy Spirit needs to be our teacher. Do you know who your teacher is, at this point of your life?

> *"But when He, the Spirit of truth, comes, He will guide you into all the truth; for He will not speak on His own initiative, but whatever He hears, He will speak; and He will disclose to you what is to come. "(John 16:13)*

> *As for you, the anointing which you received from Him abides in you, and you have no need for anyone to teach you; but as His anointing teaches you about all things, and is true and is not a lie, and just as it has taught you, you abide in Him. (I John 2:27)*

9

Who Has the Authority?

I remember something that happened to me about two years after I'd been prayed over for the baptism of the Holy Spirit. Pauline and I had opened our home to have prayer and healing meetings. I was not a pastor; I had no seminary training, neither was I well-versed in the Bible. The only thing I had going for me was that God had told me to do it.

Then we began doing these home meetings several nights a week in different towns. People were being healed, some were receiving Jesus as their personal Savior, and others were receiving the baptism of the Holy Spirit. Some of the pastors in the area became disturbed by what we were doing, so they asked me to come and have a meeting with them. But before I went, I prayed for the Lord to guide me, and He told me, "Only say what I tell you to say."

I went to this meeting; four pastors from the area were there. They had two pages of questions they began to ask me. Every time they asked me a question, the Holy Spirit would give me a Scripture to answer their question with. I answered several questions as the Holy Spirit continued to tell me what to say.

We had gone through almost a page of questions, when one of the pastors became very agitated with me. He said, "Ralph, I don't want you quoting the Scriptures. I don't want you to answer these questions with a Bible verse! I want to hear what you have to say!"

I replied, "I don't have any answers; all I know is what the Bible tells me."

The man said, "I am a theologian; I know what the Bible says!" He threw his papers on the desk and stormed out of the office, mad as a hornet. I was never asked back to another meeting.

One of the questions they'd asked me was, "Where do you get your authority from?" To answer their question I opened the Bible to Mark 16:15-18 and began reading:

And He said to them, "Go into all the world and preach the gospel to all creation. He who has believed and has been baptized shall be saved; but he who has disbelieved shall be condemned.

"And these signs will accompany those who have believed: in My name they will cast out demons, they will speak with new tongues; they will pick up serpents, and if they drink any deadly poison, it shall not hurt them; they will lay hands on the sick, and they will recover."

I was not trying to take away any pastor's authority; I was simply doing what the Holy Spirit told me to do. Interestingly, one of the things they recognized was that I did have some authority.

Another good question is: who is the authority? Who is the authority in your church? Who is the authority in your home or business? It is important to recognize that the person claiming authority is not always the one who has the authority.

Through the years of ministry, the Holy Spirit has showed me some wonderful things concerning authority. For example, God's authority is something that moves around a lot. It moves from one person to another, in our church, in our home, and in all kinds of group situations. So it is vitally important that we recognize where the authority is and who has it at any particular moment.

In the past forty years, Pauline and I have ministered at hundreds of meetings—in homes, halls, churches. What we have seen is that in some of these churches and groups, the wrong people are in the leadership positions. The gifted leaders are there alright, but they are not leading. Because they are not leading, other people who are not called to lead, but like to lead, step in and take over.

Another difficulty is that some people do not want to have the authority, while others want it all the time. It often seems like the one who does not want it is the best suited to have it.

We also see this problem of God's authority in families. In some homes, the wife has to assume all the authority, because the husband will not take it. In other homes, the husband takes all the authority and is a tyrant with it. Then in some homes, the children are telling the parents what to do; they have taken over the authority from their parents and this is not a good or healthy situation.

A godly authority moves from one person to another; the important thing is to recognize who it is resting on at any particular time. When the Lord directed me to have prayer and healing meetings in our home, I had a very difficult time at first. I realize now that I felt I didn't have the authority or the ability to do this.

Soon after we started, a young pastor began to come to our meetings. I asked him to lead the meeting and teach. He accepted, but nothing was the same. The Holy Spirit was not moving in the same way and fewer people were coming to the meetings.

After several weeks, the Holy Spirit asked me when I was going to take back the leadership and do what I was called to do. So I had to talk with this pastor and tell him I was going to take over the meeting again. He very graciously agreed and stepped back from that position. When I took the authority back, the Holy Spirit began to move again: people were being healed and filled with the Holy Spirit.

In our ministry, I had to learn both how to use the authority God had given me and when I needed to get out of the way for someone else to use it. When we did church or home meetings, I learned to ask the people who were in authority what we were allowed to do in their church or group.

Often I was told to be free and do whatever the Holy Spirit wanted me to do; I would do that! At other times I was told, "We don't want any laying on of hands or praying in the Spirit," so I would not do that. I had to recognize and respect their authority and work under it, even though I had the authority to do the meeting. The Holy Spirit expected me to recognize and respect other authorities, whether it be in a church or a home.

Many ministries, prayer groups and churches have started in the last fifty years, but some of them have already come to an end. One reason for this is the problem of recognizing Godly authority. In some groups, the wrong people took over the authority; in others, the right people would not assume the authority.

The Holy Spirit has taught me that authority is something we *must* have—in the home and in the church. If we don't have it, then we will have chaos. I have come to recognize that both Pauline and I have authority in the home. The church also has authority, and even as I have had to learn to use the authority properly, the church also has a responsibility to use its authority properly.

Why is this authority so important in the home and in the church? It is one of the things that protect the home and the church from our enemy Satan and the evil spirits. The church and God's people have been given authority over these things; if we don't use it, we are constantly defeated. If it is misused, we're still defeated.

We have seen so many Christian homes suffer loss, because the husband will not assume the spiritual authority God has given him, and the wife has to take the position as spiritual head of the household. We have seen the same thing in some churches. Men will not assume the spiritual position they should be in, and as a result, women have to assume that spiritual position in the home and in the church. Thank God they do! But it is not the best situation.

In the home, the children know something isn't right. In the church, when men refuse to take the leadership positions, women will take the leadership, and, at times men will stop coming to church, and you will have only women in the church.

In the home and in the church, both men and women need to use their authority properly. If we do, there is peace and harmony. The enemy does not have an opportunity, and we have a very fruitful environment.

May God give every one of us discernment to know when we need to take authority and when we need to relinquish it to someone else!

10

I Came to Serve

The imagination is a wonderful thing; I have had a great imagination ever since I can remember. Our ability to imagine is such a blessing from God, but of course it is like all our other abilities: it can be used for good or for evil. Soon after I received the Holy Spirit, the Lord began to use my imagination to teach me some wonderful things and to show me some things about myself that I really didn't want to see.

One day I was sitting in my living room when the Lord spoke to me and said, "I want you to imagine a great banquet hall with all the people you have known seated at a long table."

I answered, "Yes, Lord, I can imagine that."

Then He told me, "You are to have them all in this order: the person who you esteem the most, put at the head of the table; the person who you look down on, put at the foot of the table."

"Yes, Lord, I can imagine that," I responded.

The Lord continued, "Now go to the table and choose a place to sit, so that all those who you esteem as higher than yourself are toward the head of the table, and all those who you esteem as less than yourself are seated toward the foot of the table. Where would you sit?"

I would like all of you who are reading this to try something. Using your imagination, imagine the same thing I did. Imagine yourself coming into the room, then pick the place where everyone who you esteem is higher than yourself sits above you, and all those who you esteem lower, below you. Where would you sit?"

My answer to the Lord was, "Half-way." What is your answer?

The Lord then said to me, "Did you ever notice it is easier to serve those who you esteem higher than yourself, than it is to serve those who you esteem less than yourself?"

I said, "Yes, Lord, I have noticed that."

The Lord continued, "What if you came home late one night very tired, and you received a call from one of these people who you esteem higher, asking you to go out of your way for them. Would you do it?"

I said, "Of course I would!"

He said, "What if one of those from far down at the bottom, who you do not esteem, called. Would you do it?"

I answered, "I would try to make excuses as to why I couldn't help them." I began to feel very uncomfortable; I was beginning to see things I really didn't want to see.

The next question the Lord asked me was, "Where is your family seated?"

This was a shock to me. My family was seated just below me; I had esteemed them less than myself. No wonder I had such a hard time to serve them. By this time I was in tears and cried out, "God, what a wretched man I am; my heart is so small and limited."

Then the Lord said to me: "I came to serve, not to recline."

I was getting the message!

He continued: "I have not called you to recline at the table. You are to serve the whole table, from the greatest to the least. Do you know who that person is who is seated at the foot of the table? Can you lay down your life for the least of them?"

I looked at the least one, at the bottom of the table; I knew who it was, and I did not esteem that person at all. In fact, I despised that person.

The Lord explained to me: "I died for that person; I love that person. I gave my all for that person and I want you to do the same thing."

On that day, I saw things about myself I needed to see, and I have never forgotten it.

Jesus said, "You will know the truth, and the truth will set you free." A lot of the truth that we need to see is our own sad condition.

We are called to follow in His footsteps and to serve!

11

Story of Two Trees

The two trees in the garden of Eden are very important to us, because we have to make the same choices Adam and Eve did: which tree are we going to eat from?

> *And the LORD God planted a garden toward the east, in Eden; and there He placed the man whom He had formed.*
> *And out of the ground the LORD God caused to grow every tree that is pleasing to the sight and good for food; the tree of life also in the midst of the garden, and the tree of the knowledge of good and evil. (Genesis 2:8-9)*

The Lord God made it very clear what would happen to Adam if he ate from the tree of the knowledge of good and evil: He was going to die! That tree was deadly poison!

> *Then the LORD God took the man and put him into the garden of Eden to cultivate it and keep it. And the LORD God commanded the man, saying, "From any tree of the garden you may eat freely; but from the tree of the knowledge of good and evil you shall not eat, for in the day that you eat from it you will surely die." (Genesis 2:15-17)*
>
> *Now the serpent was more crafty than any beast of the field which the LORD God had made. And he said to the woman, "Indeed, has God said, 'You shall not eat from any tree of the garden?'"*
> *And the woman said to the serpent, "From the fruit of the trees of the garden we may eat; but from the fruit of the tree which is in the middle of the garden, God has said, 'You shall not eat from it or touch it, lest you die.'"*
> *And the serpent said to the woman, "You surely shall not die! For God knows that in the day you eat from it your eyes will be opened, and you will be like God, knowing good and evil."*
> *When the woman saw that the tree was good for food, and that it was a delight to the eyes, and that the tree was desirable to make one wise, she took from its fruit and ate; and she gave also to her husband with*

her, and he ate. (Genesis 3:1-6).

When Adam and Eve ate fruit from the tree of the knowledge of good and evil, evil entered into them, and it has been with us ever since. I've heard people say, "I am a good person!" Yes, but remember the fruit was both good and evil, so within every one of us is the capability of doing good and evil.

The Apostle Paul was aware of this possibility when he wrote in Romans 7:19-21:

> *For the good that I wish, I do not do, but I practice the very evil that I do not wish. But if I am doing the very thing I do not wish, I am no longer the one doing it, but sin which dwells in me. I find then the principle that evil is present in me, the one who wishes to do good.*

Where did this sin and evil come from? When did it enter in? It came from the tree of knowledge of good and evil. When Adam and Eve ate the fruit, it entered into them, and became a part of them; it has been with us ever since.

It is right in our flesh. This is why our body can't be taken up when we die; the body is defiled. Thank God, because of what Jesus did on the cross, our soul and spirit can rise with Him.

You may have noticed that anytime we allow the "old man"—the natural man, the flesh—to have its way, sin happens. If we want to rise above it, we must function as spiritual men and women.

There was another tree in the garden, the tree of life, and now because of what Jesus Christ did for us on the cross, this tree is available to us once more.

When we turn to Jesus and receive Him in our lives, something wonderful happens. We have what Jesus called a born–again experience or what some churches call a conversion experience. When this experience happens to us, we come alive spiritually and become a new creation.

You may be a Catholic and decide to become a Baptist, but this does not mean you have had a conversion or a born-again experience—you have just become a convert. Simply changing churches does not make you a child of God or a new creation.

Jesus was the first born of the new creation. When He was born of the flesh through Mary, He became God and man combined into one new being, the new Adam. When we receive Jesus Christ into our lives, we become a new creation too: Jesus and man combined into one new being. Now as a new creation (man and spirit), we can boldly go right to the tree of life and partake of it.

But the sad mistake we make is that we want to know everything, and we go right back to the tree of knowledge of good and evil, instead of going to Jesus and the tree of life.

What is so deadly about this tree of knowledge of good and evil? The whole tree is poison to us! This tree has a lot of branches and limbs; some of them are bad and some of them good, but they are all on the same tree. The whole tree is rotten, not just the bad branches and limbs. The good branches and limbs are rotten too!

Say we have a wonderful conversion experience with Jesus and the Holy Spirit. One of the first things that happens is we begin to see some of the sinful things in our life. We quickly confess them and try not to do them anymore; but to our surprise, they seem to keep cropping up and we have to keep cutting them off. What we are not seeing is that we are keeping the good limbs; by only cutting off the bad limbs, we are allowing the tree of knowledge of good and evil to live.

The Bible refers to these good limbs as a bunch of "dirty rags." The Apostle Paul referred to them as "dung." When we look at ourselves and think, "I am a pretty good person, I'm not as bad as that guy over there," we are not seeing what we truly are. Paul called himself, "the greatest of sinners." What we are doing is judging ourselves by the tree of knowledge, by our natural thinking, not by God's Word!

We don't need all the answers anymore; all we need is the tree of life. We can become great theologians, know the Bible from end to end, but still be eating from the tree of knowledge of good and evil, the tree that kills us every time, instead of partaking of the tree of life.

Jesus Christ is the tree of life. He is the living Word that comes down from heaven: eat from Him and you will live!

12

Why the Ten Commandments?

The Ten Commandments have been a problem for many people, starting with the Israelites. What was their problem? They couldn't keep them. What about the church today? We have the same problem as they did; we can't keep them either.

What is the primary purpose of the Ten Commandments? Their primary purpose is to open our eyes so that we can see the sin we live in. What is it we are to see? If we take a good look at the Commandments (also called the Law), we can see that we have failed and have a lot of problems.

I have asked many people if they thought the Ten Commandments were good. Every one of them said *yes*! Some of these people were Christians and some were not. Why would they all say yes? Because the Ten Commandments put a vision of holiness in our very soul, and we agree with that vision and say, "Yes, this is the way to live!"

We are even taught to live by this "golden rule," but when we try to live by it, we keep failing over and over. When we compare all the things we say and do and use the Ten Commandments to measure ourselves by, we fall far short of perfection. And if we should have some success, we become self-righteous and prideful—and that is sinful too.

Then why did God give us these commandments that are impossible to follow? To give us a knowledge of sin!

> *Now we know that whatever the Law says, it speaks to those who are under the Law, that every mouth may be closed, and all the world may become accountable to God; because by the works of the Law no flesh will be justified in His sight; for through the Law comes the knowledge of sin. (Romans 3:19-20)*

I was blind and now I see! Thank God I now have a knowledge of sin. There are a lot of people in the world who do not believe they are sinners. Many of them are in our churches and may be members of our family.

Some people react quite strongly when you imply they are sinners. This really ruffles their ire, and they respond by saying, "I am not a sinner!" A person who says that is still blind, unaware they are sinners, and that Jesus Christ died on the cross to cover their sin.

> *As it is written, "There is none righteous, not even one; there is none who understands, there is none who seek for God; All have turned aside, together they have become useless; there is none who does good, there is not even one."*
>
> *"Their throat is an open grave, with their tongues they keep deceiving, the poison of asps is under their lips; whose mouth is full of cursing and bitterness; their feet are swift to shed blood; destruction and misery are in their paths, and the path of peace they have not known. There is no fear of God before their eyes." (Romans 3:10-18)*

The Ten Commandments were given to Moses, before Jesus came, so that we could see ourselves as sinners and realize we need a Savior. What good would it have done to send a Savior, if nobody could see a need for one?

> *And Jesus said, "For judgment I came into this world, that those who do not see may see, and that those who see may become blind." Those of the Pharisees who were with Him heard these things and said to Him, "We are not blind too, are we?"*
>
> *Jesus said to them, "If you were blind, you would have no sin; but since you say, 'We see,' your sin remains." (John 9:39-41)*

The person who says, "I don't need Jesus!" is blind and all their sin remains—even if they try to keep the commandments or go to church every day, no matter what church they go to. They may be a pastor or a minister, but this is not the issue. The issue is that man has fallen, and only Jesus Christ and the cross can bring us back into the right relationship with God.

Trying to keep the Ten Commandments, going to church, or being a priest or pastor does not pay the price for your sin; only

Jesus Christ does. The Apostle Paul touched upon this issue in 1 Corinthians 2:2:

> *For I determined to know nothing among you except Jesus Christ, and Him crucified.*

Thank God for the Ten Commandments that make us aware of our sin and of our need of Jesus Christ.

13

The Letter of the Law

Who also made us adequate as servants of a new covenant, not of the letter but of the Spirit; for the letter kills, but the Spirit gives life.—2 Corinthians 3:6

Laws are good things. We need laws in our lives; without laws, we would be lawless. I would not want to live in a lawless country. I wouldn't want to drive or walk through any of our major cities in this country, if we did not have laws and the police to enforce them.

Both the Old Covenant and the New Covenant are law systems. The Old Covenant was laws written on tablets of stone, which is external. The New Covenant is written on the tablets of the human heart, which is internal.

The Apostle Paul had a better understanding of these two covenants than any of the other people of his day. He was picked by God to teach and help us understand the New Covenant so we could function as New Testament Christians.

He was chosen for this work because of his background in serving the Old Covenant and the letter of the law; Paul understood how deadly the law was, the bondage it brought people under. I believe Paul had a better understanding of the New Covenant than any of the other apostles, because he had experienced Jesus after He was resurrected and became the King of Kings; he was no longer a natural man. Also Paul had been taken up into the heavens where he saw and experienced things he could not share.

After his Damascus road experience, Paul spent the rest of his life teaching the New Covenant and setting people free from the letter of the law and man's religion, teaching them to function as spiritual men and women.

Paul's words always amaze me, because he was one of the top teachers in Israel. Look at how he described himself:

> *And when I came to you, brethren, I did not come with superiority of speech or of wisdom, proclaiming to you the testimony of God. For I determined to know nothing among you except Jesus Christ, and Him crucified. (1 Corinthians 2:1-2)*

You'd think of all people, Paul could rely on his vast knowledge and wisdom to reach people for Christ. Yet when he was blinded physically and his spiritual eyes were opened, he realized that, with all his vast knowledge and wisdom, he'd not been able to recognize Jesus Christ as the Savior when He walked on this earth.

Notice that in his ministry, Paul did *not* spend a lot of time attacking sin; he attacked the letter of the law and worldly religion, instead. I discovered in my own experience that, if we become free of the letter of the law and man's religion, many of our sin problems are gone! Why? Because the law is what gives sin power in our lives: the letter of the law locks us into our sin, and we can't get free from it. The letter of the law blinds us, but the Spirit opens our eyes.

Jesus told a story about a man traveling on a road, the Good Samaritan. I think this is such a wonderful story because it shows us the difference between the letter of the law and the Spirit of the law.

> *Jesus replied and said, "A certain man was going down from Jerusalem to Jericho; and he fell among robbers, and they stripped him and beat him, and went off leaving him half dead. And by chance a certain priest was going down on that road, and when he saw him, he passed by on the other side. And likewise a Levite also, when he came to the place and saw him, passed by on the other side.*
>
> *But a certain Samaritan, who was on a journey, came upon him; and when he saw him, he felt compassion, and came to him and bandaged up his wounds, pouring oil and wine on them; and he put him on his own beast, and brought him to an inn, and took care of him. And on the next day he took out two denarii, and gave them to the innkeeper*

and said, 'Take care of him; and whatever more you spend, when I return, I will repay you.'" (Luke 10:30-36)

Which of these three men do you think proved to be a neighbor to the man who'd fallen into the robbers' hands?

And he said, "The one who showed mercy toward him." And Jesus said to him, "Go and do the same." (Luke 10:37)

The priest and the Levite had no understanding of what it meant to fulfill the "royal law of love" (James 2:8). All they knew how to do was to fulfill the letter of the law that is comprised of keeping the laws, rules, and traditions. They did not understand the Spirit of the law. They were just as blind as Paul was before the scales fell from his eyes. They were in the same condition as he was before he had his Damascus road experience—he'd been stoning Christians and putting them in prison.

Why didn't the priest and the Levite stop and care for the wounded man? They were so bound by the letter of the law—their laws, rules and man's religion—that they were unable to stop.

Why did the Samaritan stop? Because his heart and spirit would not allow him to go by without doing everything possible to help the man.

Who also made us adequate as servants of a new covenant, not of the letter, but of the Spirit; for the letter kills, but the Spirit gives life. (2 Corinthians 3:6).

I had a wonderful experience a while back. I was out walking and the Lord brought to mind the Good Samaritan parable. As I was thinking about this parable, the Lord told me the difference between the Good Samaritan and the priest and the Levite: one understood the difference between the letter of the law and the spirit of the law, and the others didn't.

He then said something to me that shocked me. He said, "You have become religious."

I replied, "Lord, I don't think I am religious; I don't think I was ever religious."

He responded, "Yes, you have become religious, but not like the priest and the Levite. You have become religious, because you have begun to care for people." Then He brought to my mind this Scripture:

> *This is pure and undefiled religion in the sight of our God and Father, to visit orphans and widows in their distress, and to keep oneself unstained by the world. (James 1:27)*

Then I understood what He was trying to show me in that parable. The Good Samaritan had the spiritual law of love written in his heart; the priest and the Levite only understood the letter of the law and were trying their best to keep it.

A while back I was sharing this teaching. When I finished, a woman spoke up and asked if she could share something that had happened to her a few days before.

This is what she shared: "That message really spoke to me. My daughter is a hair-dresser, and last Sunday morning when we were getting ready for church, the phone rang. My daughter answered the phone, and I heard her say, 'Yes, of course I can do that; I will be right over.'

"Then she told me that a woman needed her hair fixed, and she started getting her stuff ready to go. I couldn't believe she was going to go fix someone's hair when it was time to go to church, and I told her so! But she said, 'Mother, this woman just came out of the hospital and she needs her hair done; I am going to do it for her.' She picked up her stuff and left. I was upset with her, putting this woman's hairdo ahead of church.

"The next day she told me what had happened. As she was fixing this sick woman's hair, my daughter started telling her about Jesus. The woman accepted Jesus as her Savior, and my daughter prayed with her for healing and to be filled with the Holy Spirit. This woman died very soon after."

Church is very important; I would not want anyone to think it isn't. But what the priest and the Levite failed to see was that people who are in distress and hurting are more important than how often we are in church, our rules and traditions, or if we get to church on time.

Another comment Jesus made was that a mule stuck in a mud hole was more important than many other things. Pure and undefiled religion puts the needs of people first.

The priest and the Levite were keepers of the letter of the law and would never notice a mule stuck in the mud. The Good Samaritan saw the need of the man in the ditch, and he also would have pulled the mule out of the mud!

There is a big difference between the letter of the law that kills and the Spirit of the law that gives life: one ministers life, the other death. Which one of these do you serve? The letter of the law or the Spirit of the law?

14

A Dream – The Spiritual Library

I had the following dream one night. In my dream someone is walking with me along a sidewalk. We come up to this large, impressive building with wide marble steps going up to large double doors at the top. When we got to the steps, instead of going up the stairs, this person led me around the side of the stairs to a small door; we entered into the door and took the steps down.

At the bottom of the steps, there was another door; a large angel was guarding the door with a sword, stopping anyone from entering the room. I hesitated, but the person with me led me on into the room, and the angel did not stop us.

Upon entering the room, I was amazed; it was filled with books. All the walls had shelves that were filled to the ceiling with books. There were tables and stands all around covered with books, too. There were other tables where people could sit, and those tables were also covered with books.

At this point I realized I was in a library, but apart from the books and the tables, the room was empty: no people were there. I was also aware that upstairs there was a large library, and many people were up there.

I then began to glance at the books around me and wonder what they were about. Some of the books were open; I noticed they were all about the Holy Spirit, the gifts of the Holy Spirit, and the fruit of the Holy Spirit. There also were books on the power and authority of the Holy Spirit, books on knowing and hearing God's voice, and books on developing a relationship with Jesus. I realized they were all spiritual books.

Somehow I had a knowing that upstairs it was all religious books, and there were many people studying and learning religious things up there. Downstairs, the books were all spiritual, but the place was empty—the angel at the door with a sword was not letting anyone pass into this room, unless they were on a spiritual journey with Christ.

When I woke up, I spent a lot of time thinking about my dream and what it meant. This is what the Lord showed me: many people are practicing religion, but not many are spiritual. The angel with the flaming sword does not let anyone enter and learn these spiritual truths, unless they turn to Jesus for salvation and have a true conversion, a born-again experience.

The upper floor represents us trying to reach God through the natural mind and reasoning, by the outward practice of religion. The room underneath represents us approaching God from the heart and spirit, learning to function as spiritual men and women.

Remember the angel and the flaming sword that were placed at the entrance to the Garden of Eden? That angel was keeping anyone from re-entering the Garden and partaking of the tree of life. God was not going to allow any one to partake of that tree unless they come through His Son, Jesus Christ; only then can we get by that angel with the flaming sword and partake of the spiritual banqueting table.

The question is: which floor are we spending our time in? The upper floor is the letter of the law that binds us and makes us work hard to earn our way into heaven; it is the external practice of religion. The lower floor is where the Spirit gives life and liberty and sets us free; it is the internal practice of being spiritual and having a close intimate walk with God.

One of the Scriptures I really enjoy is 2 Corinthians 3:1-6:

> *Are we beginning to commend ourselves again? Or do we need, as some, letters of commendation to you or from you? You are our letter, written in our hearts, known and read by all men; being manifested that you are a letter of Christ, cared for by us, written not with ink, but with the Spirit of the living God, not on tablets of stone, but on tablets of human hearts.*

And such confidence we have through Christ toward God. Not that we are adequate in ourselves to consider anything as coming from ourselves, but our adequacy is from God, who also made us adequate as servants of a new covenant, not of the letter, but of the Spirit; for the letter kills, but the Spirit gives life.

Part Two

Spiritual Revelation

15

Born to Slavery

The question is: have you ever struggled with sin? I expect most of you would say *yes*. Have you been defeated over and over again by sin and wondered why? The answer may be that you are a slave to sin.

The next question might be: how in the world do we get free from slavery to sin? There is only one way: the old sin nature in us must be put to death. This is done by us joining Jesus Christ on the cross.

How do we join Jesus Christ on the cross? We join Him on the cross through a very simple little act of being baptized with water and applying our faith.

Dying to sin is a faith issue. When we receive communion, do we have to apply faith? Of course we do; otherwise it is just another ritual. When we receive a blessing from a priest or minister, do we have to apply faith? Again, the answer is yes! When we go through the waters of baptism, do we also have to apply faith? The answer is yes! Our entire Christian walk is based on acts of faith.

What must I believe? I must believe that, when I am baptized, I am joining Jesus Christ on the cross, where He died for my sins.

You might ask, "How come I still sin? I have been baptized." It is because you are allowing the old nature to be active in you. You can no longer use the excuse that you were born to sin, because through baptism you have been set free from the bondage to sin. However, there are some sins we like, or they have become habitual, so we keep right on doing them.

Receiving Jesus as our Savior gives us the opportunity to start our life over again, to be born again, not to sin and bondage, but to righteousness and freedom from sin. Our mind does not want to believe that we can live a holy, godly life without sin. We can! Because God, through Jesus Christ, has given us everything we need to live a life of victory over sin.

In Romans 6, the Apostle Paul did such a wonderful job of explaining how to deal with the sin problem through baptism, when we are united with the death of Jesus on the cross:

> *What shall we say then? Are we to continue in sin that grace may increase? May it never be! How shall we who died to sin still live in it? (Romans 6:1-2)*

In this Scripture, Paul is telling us that we have died to sin! Now, the question is: "Have I died to sin, or am I still alive to sin?" If sin is still very active in me, then somehow I have missed or not understood what he is talking about. I believe there are a lot of people who do not understand what baptism is for.

One of the things I have heard often is that public baptism is a testimony, showing that we have received Jesus as our Lord and Savior. For others, it is a sign we have become a Catholic, Baptist, or Pentecostal—a member of a church.

Have you ever wondered why there are so many mixed-up people in the church? Why do so many Christian families fall apart? Why do so many pastors, priests, and ministers have such sin problems? The Bible answers this question by telling us that we have not laid a solid foundation (see Part Three: The Spiritual Foundation).

If a person asks Jesus Christ into their heart, joins a church and becomes real active in it, or even becomes a priest or minister, does this mean they have laid a good spiritual foundation? No! Our spiritual foundation is a lot more than becoming a church member in good standing.

> *Or do you not know that all of us who have been baptized into Christ Jesus have been baptized into His death. Therefore we have been buried with Him through baptism into death, in order that as Christ was raised from the dead through the glory of the Father, so we too might walk in newness of life. (Romans 6:3-4)*

Newness of life is the issue here. The victory we have in Christ is because the old sinful nature is put to death. As long as the sinful nature remains alive in us, we have a big problem. Paul is telling us that death is involved with water baptism.

Our walk with God is a walk of life and death. Resurrection does not happen without death first. When we receive Jesus as our Lord and Savior, we are receiving Life: we become a new creation. When we go through the water of baptism, we die—the old man is put to death. In a simple little act of faith, we are joining Jesus Christ in His death on the cross.

How does this happen? As we go through water baptism, we must apply our faith and believe that through this simple little act, we are going back over two thousand years and being nailed right on the cross with Jesus.

I prayed for God to give me a revelation of this act; then I saw a picture of the cross with Jesus nailed on it. It was like Jesus was made of plywood, with many layers, and every layer was a different person.

I asked the Lord what this meant. He explained, "Every person who has been baptized with water and applied faith to that act was nailed on that cross with Me, and their old sin nature died there with Me."

The question is, how many people know and believe this?

Or do you not know that all of us who have been baptized into Christ Jesus have been baptized into His death. (Romans 6:3)

So many Christian people are defeated, day after day, in so many ways. The Bible tells us, "My people are destroyed for lack of knowledge." In another place it says, "You will know the truth and the truth will set you free." Time after time, we suffer loss, because we lack truth and knowledge in many areas of our lives.

Another Scripture says, "The blind lead the blind and they all fall in the ditch." Who was Jesus talking about? The leaders of that time—the Scribes, Pharisees, Sadducees, and Priests—and the people who were blindly following them.

Was he also talking about us? Do we have any blind leaders, today? Of course we do—in the government, the world, our churches, our homes. When our lives and marriages are falling apart, we should ask ourselves, *what is wrong*?

We need to take a good look at our Christian foundation and see if it is well laid! Not only was the old sin nature nailed on the cross with Jesus, but when He was taken down and buried, we were buried with him.

> *Therefore we have been buried with Him through baptism into death, in order that as Christ was raised from the dead through the glory of the Father, so we too might walk in newness of life. (Romans 6:4)*

We must believe that we were nailed on the cross with Jesus and died with Him. We must also believe we were *buried* with Him in the tomb and rose from the dead into newness of life.

Do we walk in newness of life? Most of us do not; we continue to say and do the same old things that hurt and injure people day after day. Why do we do this? We do this because we are slaves to sin. We need to experience resurrection so that we can walk in newness of life. Paul continues to explain this truth in Romans 6:5-11:

> *For if we have become united with Him in the likeness of His death, certainly we shall be also in the likeness of His resurrection; knowing this, that our old self was crucified with Him, that our body of sin might be done away with, that we would no longer be slaves to sin; for he who has died is freed from sin.*
>
> *Now if we have died with Christ, we believe that we shall also live with Him, knowing that Christ, having been raised from the dead, is never to die again; death no longer is master over Him.*
>
> *For the death that He died, He died to sin, once for all; but the life that He lives, He lives to God. Even so consider yourselves to be dead to sin, but alive to God in Christ Jesus.*

This is such a wonderful teaching from Paul. I encourage you to open your Bible and read Romans 6 over and over, until you really understand what he was trying to teach us.

There is one thing we must understand: even though the old

sin nature is dead, we can still sin. However, we no longer have the excuse that we had to do it, because we are no longer slaves to sin. We now sin because we want to. We gossip because we like to! We say bad things from our mouth because we want to hurt people! We do some bad things because we love to do them!

When we come to hate sin, we will turn away from it. May God help us to love life and hate evil. There is a saying in the Bible we should all pay attention to: "A wise man turns away from sin and evil" (see Proverbs 14:16).

16

Open Our Eyes, Lord

Paul, formerly known as Saul, was a great teacher in Israel, but he had one serious problem: he was blind and didn't know it. Paul was not the only one who was blind; the rest of the Jews were also blind. Even after his eyes were opened, Paul knew that he still did not see very clearly. He said, "I see as through a dark colored glass dimly."

I also have to say the same thing: "I see, but dimly!" I am sure some of you would like to say that you see clearly, but I don't believe you; you also see dimly.

The Apostle Paul had a very special ministry to the Jews and to the Gentiles—this includes you and me today. Even though Paul saw dimly, he had a greater understanding of the New Covenant, more than any of the other New Testament writers; this is still true today.

Paul understood how deadly the letter of the law is, and how life-giving the Spirit of the law is. His teachings in the New Testament have set many people free from the letter of the law—"you shall know the truth, and the truth shall make you free" (John 8:32).

Paul was called by God for a very specific purpose; this purpose is best described in his own words in Acts 26:15-18:

> *And I said, "Who art Thou, Lord?" And the Lord said, "I am Jesus whom you are persecuting.*
>
> *But arise, and stand on your feet; for this purpose I have appeared to you, to appoint you a minister and a witness not only to the things which you have seen, but also to the things in which I will appear to you; delivering you from the Jewish people and from the Gentiles, to whom I am sending you, to open their eyes so that they may turn from darkness to light and from the dominion of Satan to God, in order that they may receive forgiveness of sins and an inheritance*

among those who have been sanctified by faith in me."

It is important to understand that, before Paul was knocked to the ground by a light from heaven and blinded, he was a prisoner to the letter of the law. He was bound to the Old Covenant, without any understanding of the New Covenant; in fact, he was very zealous in trying to destroy the early church.

When Paul was trying to destroy the new believers, he was convinced he was serving God and doing the right thing. Killing and putting them in prison was not a sin to him; he was blind, unable to see beyond the letter of the law written in stone. He considered himself blameless.

After he was called by Jesus, Paul could have boasted about his background, yet he didn't. Here is what he said:

> *Although I myself might have confidence even in the flesh. If anyone else has a mind to put confidence in the flesh, I far more: circumcised the eighth day, of the nation of Israel, of the tribe of Benjamin, a Hebrew of Hebrews; as to the Law, a Pharisee; as to zeal, a persecutor of the church; as to righteousness which is in the Law, found blameless. But whatever things were gain to me, those things I have counted as loss for the sake of Christ. (Philippians 3:4-7)*

Why did Paul say he considered all those things as loss for the sake of Christ? What did Paul see that had changed his mind? He saw that there wasn't any power in any of the law to change a person's life.

Although we may be able to keep some laws and be very diligent in practicing our religion, none of this can change us—only the law of life in Christ Jesus has the power to change us!

The Bible tells us to repent; this was spoken to God's people. Repentance means that we are going the wrong way and we need to change our direction.

God is not looking for people who are bound by rules and regulations; He is looking for people who will walk with Him, enjoy being with Him, and have an intimate relationship with Him.

Many years ago my local priest told me he observed that, over a period of time, his congregation was changing; half of them were becoming more holy, the other half more wicked.

What was going on? Half of them had Christ and the Holy Spirit at work in them, and as a result, repentance was happening—they were changing. The other half were practicing religion, but they did not have a relationship with Jesus Christ. They were in the same condition as Paul was before his conversion—a practice of religion, with no power in it.

Paul was the perfect man for the work and ministry God called him into; he understood the letter of the law, and he could see from his past just how deadly it was to him and to the whole nation of Israel. If we can see this, we will understand why Paul spoke as he did to the Corinthians:

> *And when I came to you, brethren, I did not come with superiority of speech or of wisdom, proclaiming to you the testimony of God. For I determined, to know nothing among you except Jesus Christ and Him crucified. (1 Corinthians 2:1-2)*

A number of years ago, a friend of mine was dying of cancer and I was asked to go to the nursing home to see if I could encourage him to ask Christ into his life. He was very close to death. A few days later I went to visit him.

I asked him, "Have you ever received Jesus Christ as your Savior?"

He replied, "No!" He explained to me that he had been a good person all his life. He had helped many people, belonged to many good organizations, worked with the Boy Scouts and Girl Scouts for many years, and gave freely to those in need. He was a church member and he supported the church.

He then said, "Certainly, God is not going to reject me!" I wonder how many people in the world think the same thing, the same way: *God is not going to reject me!*

I prayed and asked the Lord to help me reach him. The Holy Spirit told me to tell him that all his good works were a bunch of dirty rags. I knelt down by his bed, looked right in his eyes, and said, "All your good works are a bunch of dirty rags."

His eyes got real big and he began to sob. When he was able to get his breath and was able to speak, the first thing that came out of his mouth was, “I need Jesus Christ!” He asked Jesus into his heart, and the next day he died.

God opened the eyes of his heart, and he saw the sad condition his soul was in. May God show every one of us our sad condition, and may we see our need of a Savior.

17

The Work of Jesus Christ

Jesus has been called by many titles—the Son of God, the Lamb of God, Savior, and our High Priest. He was also referred to as "the first born of the new creation." Another one of His titles is the new Adam: where the old Adam failed, the new one did not. He fulfilled the law, but He did not do this for His own benefit; He did it for our benefit.

In Hebrews 1:1-3, Jesus is described in this way:

God, after He spoke long ago to the fathers in the prophets in many portions and in many ways, in these last days has spoken to us in His Son, whom He appointed heir of all things, through whom also He made the world.

And He is the radiance of His glory and the exact representation of His nature, and upholds all things by the word of His power. When He had made purification of sins, He sat down at the right hand of the Majesty on high.

The work of Jesus Christ was to remove the barrier between God and man; the barrier was sin. In order to remove this barrier, Jesus had to become the spotless lamb, without a blemish, and be offered as a sacrifice for our sins.

He chose to become united with us, take our sin nature and put it to death with Him on the cross; we would be buried with Him and rise with Him to experience resurrection. If we choose to accept Jesus as our Savior and what He has done for us, we can walk in newness of life, here and in the hereafter.

We sometimes mistakenly think that all we need to do to enter the kingdom of God is to be a good church member. Wrong! We must have a conversion experience in which we are born again and become a new creation! Why? The kingdom of God is spirit! Flesh and blood cannot inherit the kingdom of God.

Many people in the church have a problem with this statement: "You must be born again." They laugh and say, "Another one of those born again people."

But if you are not born again, it doesn't matter if you are a Jew, Protestant, Catholic or any other group, you will not see the kingdom of God and you will not enter it! You might be a Rabbi, a priest, or a minister, but if you are not born again, you will not enter into it.

Jesus made this very clear when Nicodemus came to see Him:

> *Now there was a man of the Pharisees, named Nicodemus, a ruler of the Jews; this man came to Jesus by night, and said to Him, "Rabbi, we know that You have come from God as a teacher; for no one can do these signs that You do unless God is with him."*
>
> *Jesus answered and said to him, "Truly, truly, I say to you, unless one is born again he cannot see the kingdom of God."*
>
> *Nicodemus said to Him, "How can a man be born when he is old? He cannot enter a second time into his mother's womb and be born, can he?"*
>
> *Jesus answered, "Truly, truly, I say to you, unless one is born of water and the Spirit he cannot enter into the kingdom of God. That which is born of the flesh is flesh, and that which is born of the Spirit is spirit. Do not marvel that I said to you, 'You must be born again.'" (John 3:1-7)*

These Scriptures make it very clear. We cannot see the kingdom of God or enter the kingdom of God without being born again. It is a spiritual kingdom, and thus we must be spiritual to enter it. Remember Paul, as religious as he was, could not see or enter the kingdom of God until he had the Damascus road conversion experience.

In the Old Covenant, there was a place called the Holy of Holies. Only the high priest could enter it once a year, but he had to take blood, as an offering for himself and for the sins of the people, when he entered it.

Jesus our high priest entered the Holy of Holies; it was His blood He offered, as the perfect offering for our sins, when He died on the cross. Remember when He died, the veil to the Holy of Holies was torn from the top to the bottom, signifying that the way was now open for us. Through the death of Jesus Christ, our High Priest, we can go boldly to the throne of grace, right into the Holy of Holies.

Some people think there are many ways into the kingdom of God. Listen to what Jesus said about this: "I am the way, and the truth, and the life; no one comes to the Father but through Me." (John 14:6)

If you believe otherwise, you believe a lie!

John the Baptist prepared the way for the coming of Jesus. Jesus prepared the way for the coming of the Holy Spirit; it was not until Jesus ascended into Heaven that the promise of the Holy Spirit would come. Before that time, only a few special people had the Holy Spirit come down on them. Now all of us can experience the Holy Spirit, if we will go to Jesus first, and then ask Him to baptize us with the Holy Spirit.

Remember, the public ministry of Jesus did not begin until the Holy Spirit came down upon Him, after He was baptized by John.

> *And after being baptized, Jesus went up immediately from the water; and behold, the heavens were opened, and he saw the Spirit of God descending as a dove, and coming upon Him, and behold, a voice out of the heavens, saying, "This is My beloved Son, in whom I am well-pleased." (Matthew 3:16)*

Another work of Jesus was to set us free. There is freedom for every person who wants it.

One day, as I was sitting quietly and thinking about some of the people who had asked for prayer concerning bondage to smoking and other things, the Lord gave me a vision of a man in jail. He was standing at a window with bars on, and he was looking out at the world; he had both hands on the bars, shaking them, wanting to get out.

The Lord said, "Look behind him." I turned and looked at the other side of the cell and the door was unlocked and wide open.

The Lord said to me: "I have already opened all the prison doors; all the man has to do is let go of the bars, turn around and walk out."

> *Jesus therefore was saying to those Jews who had believed Him, "If you abide (continue) in My word, then you are truly disciples of Mine; and you shall know the truth, and the truth shall make you free. (John 8:31-32)*

The lie gets in our mind, and we believe the lie, instead of the truth. For most smokers, the lie is: "I've got to have another smoke!" The truth is, you do not have to have another smoke, but you continue to believe the lie instead of the truth. When you are able to say, "I never need another smoke," and believe it, you are free.

What we are lacking is self-control over our body and our mind; the same thing is true with over-eating and all the other bondages. Jesus is the truth, the way, and the life, and He came to set us free.

Another work of Jesus was to give to those who would receive Him a new position of spiritual authority, as individuals, and also as the church body. This authority is very important, because now we have authority over demons and evil spirits, as well as over sickness and disease.

> *And I heard a loud voice in heaven, saying, "Now the salvation, and the power, and the kingdom of our God and the authority of His Christ have come, for the accuser of our brethren has been thrown down, who accuses them before our God day and night. And they overcame him because of the blood of the Lamb and because of the word of their testimony, and they did not love their life unto death. (Revelation 12:10-11)*

There is a great lack of knowledge concerning the authority Jesus has given us, as individuals and in the body of Christ. As Christian individuals, do we have spiritual authority in our homes, our work, and our families?

There are a great number of Christian families who are suffering defeats day after day, because they are not using the spiritual authority God has given them at home or at work.

Many people are afraid of evil spirits and demons, but evil spirits should be afraid of you!

All of these things are a part of what Jesus Christ did for us. Through the shedding of His blood and dying on the cross, Jesus Christ won the victory for us! The victory was not for Him, but for us!

I had a wonderful vision about five years after we began this ministry. The Holy Spirit was teaching me some things about setting people free from evil spirits. We seemed to have some success and some failures. I didn't like this ministry very well; every time we worked with someone with this problem, I would come under attack myself. It would take me from an hour to a couple of days to defeat the oppression and the attack on my mind.

One morning I had to drive out in the country about ten miles to do some electrical repairs in a house—I was still in the electrical business at the time. I knew nobody would be at home, because they were all at work. Before I left my house, a great fear came upon me; I was afraid of going to that house. I had the most dreadful feeling that something terrible was going to happen to me.

I started down the highway, and the closer I got to that house, the stronger the fear became. By the time I drove into the yard I was a mess. It took all the strength I had to get out of my car.

I finally got my tools and materials together and went into the house. Every door I went through, I thought someone or something was going to do something terrible to me. I had to go up into the dark attic and crawl space; I had to go down into the dark basement. All morning long this continued. I prayed and spoke Scriptures to myself, but it was all I could do to continue working.

At three o'clock in the afternoon, it finally broke; the fear and oppression were gone. I remember exactly what I was doing when it happened; I was kneeling in front of the furnace when it left. Then I had a wonderful vision I will never forget.

I was in a tremendous crowd of people. We were all looking up at a hill. On the top of the hill was a beautiful white horse; a man was sitting on the horse. The man was holding a great sword straight up over his head. All the people were shouting at Him, "You have the victory! You have the victory!"

He turned and looked down directly at me, and He said, "No! You have the victory!"

I *knew* it was true! He had won the victory, and somehow it had become mine. When I was under attack, and I had just hung in there hour after hour, without retreating or running away, the victory became mine.

Each one of us, somewhere along the way, must win the victory by applying our faith and trust in God and believing that we have the victory—not the enemy spirits. Coming to know Jesus in a personal way is a divine revelation. Coming to know the authority we have as God's people is also divine revelation.

At the time of Jesus' death, the veil in the temple was torn from top to bottom; His work was finished. A few days later, He rose into heaven to return to His Father and sit at His right hand. Now we can all go boldly into the Holy of Holies, right to the throne of grace, and receive the blessing He has won for us.

> *After this, Jesus, knowing that all things had already been accomplished, in order that the Scripture might be fulfilled, said, "I am thirsty."*
>
> *A jar full of sour wine was standing there; so they put a sponge full of the sour wine, upon a branch of hyssop, and brought it up to His mouth. When Jesus therefore had received the sour wine, He said, "It is finished!" And He bowed His head, and gave up His spirit. (John 19:28-30)*

18

The Work of the Holy Spirit

Our Father in heaven sent a Savior, Jesus Christ, and He also made a promise that He was going to send the Holy Spirit to be with us and in us. Jesus prepared the way for the Holy Spirit to come. He spoke many times about the Holy Spirit and how important the work of the Holy Spirit was going to be in our lives.

> *And gathering them together, He commanded them not to leave Jerusalem, but to wait for what the Father had promised, "Which," He said, "you heard of from Me; for John baptized with water, but you shall be baptized with the Holy Spirit not many days from now." (Acts 1:4-5)*

Is it important for us to be baptized with water and the Holy Spirit? Yes! Both are a part of our Christian foundation. They sometimes happen many years apart.

Why was it so important that the Holy Spirit come and baptize us? So we would become the witnesses. The Holy Spirit would work with us and in us, giving us power and authority, and signs and wonders would follow.

> *"but you will receive power when the Holy Spirit has come upon you; and you shall be My witnesses both in Jerusalem, and in all Judea and Samaria, and even to the remotest part of the earth." (Acts 1:8)*

The coming of the Holy Spirit is a confirmation that Jesus Christ was the acceptable offering for our sins to God! We must have the revelation of Jesus Christ and Him crucified in our own hearts, if we are to witness it to others.

The work of Jesus and the work of the Holy Spirit are both vitally important. Jesus prepares the way for us to return to a relationship with our Father God. He removes all the sin and the veil that stands between us and God. We can go to Jesus and be born again a new creation, and then the work of Jesus is done. This leaves us as a brand new spiritual baby in a spiritual realm that we don't know anything about.

From the time we are born we have a need for people to teach us how to feed ourselves and how to function in this world. The same is true in the spiritual realm: we need teachers. Our Father has provided the teachers we need, through the church as an institution and through individuals. These people can teach us only to a certain point; there we level off unless we have a greater teacher.

Jesus said, "My Father will give you another Helper," and He sent back the Holy Spirit to be our Helper. The Helper's job is to take us from being spiritual babies and bring us into spiritual maturity. The Holy Spirit brings us from darkness to the light, from living the lie to walking in the truth.

You might think this is the work of the church. Yes! The church does teach, but it is not the perfect teacher—the Holy Spirit is the perfect teacher.

> *"These things I have spoken to you, while abiding with you. But the Helper, the Holy Spirit, whom the Father will send in My name, He will teach you all things, and bring to your remembrance all that I said to you." (John 14:25-26)*

There are some Christian churches who only give lip service to the Holy Spirit. They do not trust the Holy Spirit to do His work; they feel they must do it for Him. These people think they can do a better job of leading you into truth than the Holy Spirit can. These are the ones who Jesus spoke of when He said, "The blind lead the blind, and they all fall into the ditch" (Matthew 15:14).

> *As for you, the anointing which you received from Him abides in you, and you have no need for anyone to teach you; but as His anointing teaches you about all things, and is true and is not a lie, and just as it has taught you, you abide in Him. (1 John 2:27)*

What does all this mean? It means that after you have asked Jesus Christ into your heart, and have been baptized with the

Holy Spirit, you now have a new teacher, the Holy Spirit. He will teach you all things and lead you into the truth.

> *"When the Helper comes, whom I will send to you from the Father, that is the Spirit of truth, who proceeds from the Father, He will bear witness of Me." (John 15:26)*

Jesus spent a lot of time telling us what the Holy Spirit would do for us. In John 14:16-17, He said:

> *"And I will ask the Father, and He will give you another Helper, that He may be with you forever; that is the Spirit of truth, whom the world cannot receive, because it does not behold Him or know Him, but you know Him because He abides with you, and will be in you."*

Do we need help? Does the church need help? Do our families need help? Yes, to all the above.

What about this Spirit of truth? Do we need Him? If we are ever to walk in the truth, we do. People can tell you some truth about yourself, but you cannot believe it and you get offended by them. However, the Holy Spirit can show you that same truth, in a way that you can receive it, and you know it is true. The Holy Spirit knows your innermost secrets; He can make you see truth when no one else can. When you see truth, it sets you free!

One of the major works of the Holy Spirit is to reveal to you the Christ who is abiding in you.

> *... that is, the mystery which has been hidden from the past ages and generations; but has now been manifested to His saints, to whom God willed to make known what is the riches of the glory of this mystery among the Gentiles, which is Christ in you, the hope of glory. (Colossians 1:26-27)*

Some of us spend a lot of time trying to prove we are somebody. We don't like our self so we try to be like somebody else we esteem. We run away from our self, but we can't escape this person within.

People spend their lifetime trying to find out, W*ho am I*? The Bible says, "Love your neighbor as yourself!" How can I love my neighbor when I can't stand myself? There use to be a TV show where they would say, "Will the real you stand up!"

I had a reoccurring dream for many years. I expect you have also have had dreams similar to it. In this dream something was always chasing me; I was trying to get away, but some monstrous thing was after me. I would wake up very frightened.

Somewhere along my spiritual journey, I was given a set of tapes about working with your dreams. This Catholic priest had done an extensive teaching on dreams. One of the things he had covered was, when you have one of those dreams where something is chasing you, you can turn around and confront whatever it is and ask it what it wants. He also said that sometimes we can re-enter a dream, if we pray and ask.

About a week later, I had the dream again: this terrible thing was chasing me, and I was trying to get away from it. I was very afraid. I woke up and remembered what the priest had said about re-entering a dream. So I said a prayer and asked to go back into the dream and confront the monster and find out what it wanted.

I went right back into the dream. I turned around and faced this monster that was after me and said, "Who are you? What do you want?" To my surprise, the monster changed and I was looking at myself!

Revelation entered my heart; I realized I had been running away from myself for years. I was the monster I was running away from. I have stopped running! Those dreams have not bothered me for years.

We are hidden in Christ! What does that mean? It means that when I find Christ in me, I also find out who I am; the real me is hidden in Christ. I have discovered the more I know Jesus, the more I know myself! I have stopped running away from myself and I have started to like myself.

> *Set your mind on the things above, not on the things that are on earth. For you have died and your life is hidden with Christ in God. When Christ, who is our life, is revealed, then you also will be revealed with Him in glory. (Colossians 3:2-4)*

The work of the Holy Spirit is to show us truth. He not only reveals Christ in me, He reveals the real me that is in Christ.

My heavenly Father asked me a question one day. He said, "Who am I?" I knew He wanted me to see something important. I thought about it for a couple of weeks, and then I knew what He wanted me to see. I said, "Lord, I know who you are."

Again He repeated His question: "Who am I?"

I answered, "Lord, You are who you are,"

He said, "Yes!" What it meant to me is that God is totally complete; He doesn't have to be anything other than who He is.

Then He asked, "Who are you?" I spent another two weeks thinking about that.

Then one day I said to Him, "Lord, I know who I am!"

He replied: "Who are you?"

I replied, "Lord, I am who I am, and I don't have to be anybody else."

He replied, "That's right."

The work of the Holy Spirit is to bring us from the darkness into the light.

> *"I have many more things to say to you, but you cannot bear them now. But when He, the Spirit of truth, comes, He will guide you into all the truth; for He will not speak on His own initiative, but whatever He hears, He will speak; and He will disclose to you what is to come. He shall glorify Me, for He shall take of Mine and shall disclose it to you." (John 16:12-14)*

Notice that the Lord has many more things to say to us, but, if we are not listening, we may not hear them. Are these things important? Yes, they are very important, because they are truths that we need to receive. Each one of these truths bring a little more light into our lives, bringing us from darkness into the light, making us a little more free.

Other people may try to show you these truths; however, it is only through the Holy Spirit that will you be able to accept them. The work of the Holy Spirit is to tell you what God is saying to you.

Jesus loved man, but He did not trust man. If you trust every person who comes along and claims to be Christian, you are foolish. People must earn your trust over a period of time; even then they will fail you at some point. The Holy Spirit can be trusted totally and completely. He does not fail us!

The work of the Holy Spirit is to glorify Jesus! When people or churches are glorifying themselves, it is not the Holy Spirit. The work of the Holy Spirit is to bring you and me into the fullness of what God created us to be.

19

The Work of the Church

To understand the work of the church, I must define what I mean by the church. I am not speaking about denominations, such as Catholic or Protestant. I am referring to the body of Christ, the spiritual organism, which is comprised of believers who have received Jesus Christ as their Savior and have had a valid conversion, a born again experience. I want to make this as clear as possible, because this is the group of people who are called and equipped to do the work of the church.

There are people in our churches who have not had a conversion, a born-again experience. You cannot expect them to do the work of the church when they are not equipped to do so. Some of you who read this may be in this condition. You desire to do the work of the church, but you lack boldness, wisdom and knowledge. Neither do you have any spiritual authority or power in your life.

What you need to do is rededicate your heart to Jesus. Ask Jesus into your heart, receive forgiveness of your sins, and ask Him to baptize you in the Holy Spirit. You can ask your church or a group of Christian people to pray over you for the fullness of the Holy Spirit and power, then you are equipped to do the work of the church.

We must also understand what the major work of the church is: it is to fulfill the great commission! In Mark 16:15, Jesus said to His followers, "Go into all the world and preach the gospel to all creation." The gospel means good news; we are to spread the good news of what Jesus Christ has done for us.

When Pauline and I began this ministry, the Lord Jesus made it very clear to us. We were not called to bring people to church, but we were to bring them to Jesus Christ. He said, "I am the One who can help them."

Pauline and I went through some very hard times in the early years of our marriage. We wanted help; we went to our priest and he talked to us and made suggestions. He even arranged for us to be involved with a Christian counseling service, and we tried that. We also talked with other folks who had similar problems, but nothing seemed to help.

However, no one had suggested we go to Jesus for help. The night before we were going to go and sign the separation papers, we both reached out to Jesus in desperation, and He saved our marriage.

As the church, our most important work is to tell others the good news that Jesus can help them: "Jesus can save you! He is the answer!"

So many people have come to us and asked us to pray for their loved ones because they are not going to church. Going to church is fine, but it is not the most important issue. We must tell them about Jesus, pray for them to know Jesus, and share Jesus with them. When they meet Jesus, they will become involved in the church—they will *be* the church!

As a Christian person, am I doing the work of bringing Jesus to others? Have I learned to introduce Jesus to people in such a way that they want to know Him?

I used to wonder about Jesus, why did He attract so many people? Well, for one thing, people were being healed and set free from demons. And I think they saw that Jesus really loved and cared for them. He also spoke with power and authority. He had life, and they were attracted to it. Jesus spoke and acted differently than the Scribes and Pharisees.

Jesus made it clear that the disciples were to wait for the Holy Spirit to come, and they would be empowered to go out and do the work of the ministry.

> *And gathering them together, He commanded them not to leave Jerusalem, but to wait for what the Father had promised, "Which," He said, "you heard of from Me; for John baptized with water, but you*

shall be baptized with the Holy Spirit not many days from now." (Acts 1:4-5)

... "but you will receive power when the Holy Spirit has come upon you; and you shall be My witnesses both in Jerusalem, and in all Judea and Samaria, and even to the remotest part of the earth." (Acts 1:8)

"Go therefore and make disciples of all the nations, baptizing them in the name of the Father and the Son and the Holy Spirit." (Matthew 28:19)

These Scriptures make it clear. We need the power of the Holy Spirit to go out into the world with the gospel, and there will be signs and wonder that follow.

And they went out and preached everywhere, while the Lord worked with them, and confirmed the word by the signs that followed. (Mark 16:20)

The work of believers in the church is to be a witness and to bring healing and deliverance out into the world to the unsaved. Most of us feel we do not have the power or authority to heal the sick or to set the captives free. If we do not have the Holy Spirit working with us, we don't! All we need to do is ask Jesus to baptize us with the Holy Spirit and empower us for the work. Jesus does not withhold any good thing from us.

One of the questions I have asked many people in the past years is, "What is God saying to you?" Very few people seem to know.

Another question I frequently asked is, "What has God called you to do?" Most people don't know.

I also ask, "What is your purpose in God's kingdom?"

Their answer, "I don't really know."

How can we fulfill our purpose if we don't know what it is? God has put us all here for a purpose! We all have a work to do; some of us are called to work in the organized church, others to work outside of the organized church. We all have a calling!

I think of the Native Americans. When a young man reached a certain age, he was sent out into the wilderness to find the vision for his life, for his purpose. I believe as Christian people we also need a vision—a vision large enough to bring us outside of our church walls and out into the world.

The work of the church is described as feeding the poor and taking care of the widows and orphans. It is finding the lost and injured sheep and bringing them back into the fold. The work of the church is doing what the Good Samaritan did—giving freely wherever there is a need, setting the captives free, opening the eyes of the blind, and doing all the things Jesus did.

The work of the church is to bring healing. "These signs will follow those who believe; they will lay hand on the sick and they shall recover." Pauline and I have been preaching this for many years, but only a few Christians believe there is healing in the hands of the church. Use those hands God has given to you. Lay them on the sick; pray for them to be healed, and see what happens.

People say, "I don't know how to pray." You don't have to know how to pray. All you have to do is have faith enough to lay your hands on the sick and believe God is healing them.

Fear of making a fool of themselves keeps many people from doing the things Jesus told us to do. God has called the church to be fools for Him; it is a privilege to be called a fool for God.

Much of the work of the church is outside the church, and there is plenty of work to go around.

> *But earnestly desire the greater gifts. And I show you a still more excellent way. (1 Corinthians 12:31)*
>
> *But now abide faith, hope, love, these three; but the greatest of these is love. (1 Corinthians 13:13)*

Do you have the kingdom of God in you? Do you have faith, hope, and love in you? The work of the church is to give all these wonderful things away. There are so many people in our churches, families, and all around us every day who are lacking in faith, hope, love, and peace. If you have any of the gifts and fruit of the Holy Spirit, they are to be given away, not hidden and stored away.

20

Our Spiritual Tool Kit

The ministry of Jesus to the public did not begin until the promise of the Father had come: the Holy Spirit. The same was true for the disciples and the New Testament Christians. The Holy Spirit would call people to the work and empower them; Paul and Barnabas were called and sent by the Holy Spirit. This appears to be a standard procedure throughout the Bible.

I think it would be impossible to separate the work of God from that of the Holy Spirit. The Holy Spirit, the third person of the God-head, is the One who is here on earth today. The Father is in Heaven, the Son is seated at His right hand in Heaven, and the Holy Spirit was sent to be with us.

It is only through the power of the Holy Spirit and the supernatural gifts of the Holy Spirit that we can effectively minister to a weary, hurting world. Apart from them, we can do nothing. If we have the fullness of the Holy Spirit in us, we have the potential for all of the gifts of the Holy Spirit to be manifested through us. Pray for the faith to use these gifts. We must have a willingness to allow the Holy Spirit to use us. We are not to control the Holy Spirit.

> *But to each one is given the manifestation of the Spirit for the common good. For to one is given the word of wisdom through the Spirit, and to another the word of knowledge according to the same Spirit; to another faith by the same Spirit, and to another gifts of healing by the one Spirit, and to another the effecting of miracles, and to another prophecy, and to another the distinguishing of spirits, to another various kinds of tongues, and to another the interpretation of tongues. (1 Corinthians 12:7-10)*

For the church to do its work, it must work with the Holy Spirit. The gifts of the Holy Spirit are for the church, so it can accomplish its work. Does a carpenter, plumber, gardener, or any other workmen need tools? Of course! The gifts of the Holy Spirit are the tools of the church; without the tools, the worker cannot accomplish the job.

I had a vision one day. I saw a man working in a garden. He was trying to shovel dirt, but he was using a hoe. Then he tried to cultivate the plants, but he used a shovel. Next, he tried to dig a hole, but he used a rake. Then he tried to clear rocks from the ground, but he used a trowel.

God gave me the interpretation of this vision. He said, "A workman must have the proper tools to do a good job. If you use the wrong tool, the job doesn't get done properly. I have not left the workmen without the proper tools. The tools that I have given to the church are the gifts of the Holy Spirit. Every worker must know how to use these tools. I want you to begin praying for the gifts of the Holy Spirit, one at a time, so you can learn how to use them."

Every job has a boss or foreman—the Holy Spirit is our foreman. He is the one who tells us what to do. Remember what Jesus said, "I only say and do what my Father tells me to." It is a good idea to become acquainted with the foreman and do what He tells you to do.

In order for the gifts to work, we need to come together as it says in the Bible: "Where two or three come together in My name, there I am in their midst" (Matthew 18:20) The very nature of the gifts requires this.

The gifts of the Holy Spirit are for the building up of the body of Christ. If you receive a word of knowledge or wisdom, it is not for you, it is for someone else. All the gifts of the Holy Spirit are for the edification of the body; the only one for personal edification is tongues. We need to learn to use these gifts properly. The Holy Spirit is our teacher; earnestly desire the greater gifts.

I have a little prayer I pray every day when we are on the road ministering: "Lord I pray for the wisdom, knowledge, discernment and faith to be able to minister properly to your people, and to those who do not know you." I know that apart from Jesus and the Holy Spirit, I have nothing to help anyone.

To have an effective ministry, we need all the gifts of the Holy Spirit. In our ministry over the years all of the gifts were manifested at one time or another as needed—tongues, interpretation, prophecy, healing, miracles, discernment of spirits, words of wisdom and knowledge.

Jesus, through the Holy Spirit, gives us all the tools we need to do all the things He did and even more.

21

Gifts of Wisdom & Knowledge

For to one is given the word of wisdom through the Spirit, and to anther the word of knowledge according to the same Spirit— 1 Corinthians 12:8

How many of us would like to be wise and knowledgeable? I expect all of us would. If you are anything like me, you realize that you have made many foolish mistakes in your lifetime.

There is a time when we honestly think we are wise and knowledgeable. We know exactly what to say and do; we have the answers for our problems and the problems of others too. After a while, we wise up and acknowledge that we don't know as much as we thought we did. When we become wise, we look to God for our answers, not to the world or to our own reasoning.

Where is the wise man? Where is the scribe? Where is the debater of this age? Has not God made foolish the wisdom of the world? (1 Corinthians 1:20)

God has chosen to manifest His power and wisdom through His Son, Jesus Christ. God, in His wisdom, knew that man could not save himself with his own efforts, in spite of his intellect and the wisdom of the world. Man was totally cut off from God's wisdom, dead in his trespasses and sin. Man did not even have the wisdom to be able to see his own sad condition.

Many today think they are wise. They think, *Look what I've accomplished. I am a leader. I have power and authority. I have done well.* But they are not wise, because they have not turned to God. They are blind leaders of the blind—and don't even know it.

But to those who are the called, both Jews and Greeks, Christ the power of God and the wisdom of God. (1 Corinthians 1:24)

I looked in a dictionary to see what it would say about wisdom. This is what the *American Heritage Dictionary* said, "understanding of what is true." This is what Jesus said: "I am the way, the truth, and the life." And I say, "Wisdom is to know and follow Jesus!"

> *The fear of the Lord is the beginning of wisdom; A good understanding have all those who do His commandments. (Psalms 111:10)*
> *And to man He said, "Behold, the fear of the Lord, that is wisdom; and to depart from evil is understanding." (Job 28:28)*

When Pauline and I started having home ministry, I did not know a thing about ministry. Nothing! The Lord had told me that He would tell me what to say and do, but I was so afraid and nervous that I lost some of my hair.

I prayed very reverently, "Lord give me the wisdom and knowledge to be able to minister to Your people in an effective way." He did. Through the word of wisdom and knowledge, miracles, healings and deliverances took place. They started in our very first meeting, and they have been happening ever since. I am still praying the same prayer today.

If we are wise, we will be discerning, weighing and testing all our thoughts, guarding our emotions, and not allowing an evil word to come out of our mouths. If we are wise, we will keep our mind and heart set on the things above and make sure we are in the kingdom of God within us. If we are wise, we will look to the wisdom of God and not to the wisdom of this world, which sounds so reasonable to our natural way of thinking.

Wisdom and humility go hand in hand. As we become wiser, we realize how little we know, and humility begins to happen.

Knowledge is very important. We should be increasing in knowledge daily, especially the knowledge of God, which comes from a relationship with Jesus and the Holy Spirit. We should have a knowledge of who and what we are in Jesus Christ. And we should be familiar with the Bible, and have a good relationship with the body of Christ, the church. We should have knowledge of the world around us too.

But when we have knowledge without wisdom, pride and arrogance can take over so easily. We have an answer for everything. We may even have the correct answer—but the wrong attitude in our heart.

Our thinking is also important. One of the books I read many years ago by George McDonald describes a young woman who had graduated from college like this: "She was filled with the thoughts of others and never learned to think for herself." A label they have for that condition today is "brain-washed." We need to learn to think for ourselves.

I enjoy thinking about many things. I like to think about what the Bible says. I also enjoy asking questions, because they make me think. I enjoy trying to break out of the box and think new thoughts.

Here's a little story I heard once. A bunch of little frogs were hopping around on a dirt road. All of a sudden, one of them disappeared. The other frogs looked around and found him in a deep rut in the road. But try as much as he could, the little frog could not jump high enough to get out of the rut. So the other frogs went their way.

After a while the missing frog joined them. They asked him, "How did you get out of the rut? He replied, 'I heard a great noise and saw a big truck tire coming at me, and I jumped out!' Sometimes we need a truck coming at us and we jump out of our rut.

Be aware that all knowledge is not good knowledge—or even truth. There are evil spirits in this world, and there are evil men in this world who distort truth and preach a lie. With God's wisdom, we are able to discern true knowledge from the lie.

22

The Gift of Faith

... to another faith by the same Spirit—1 Corinthians 12:9

The gift of faith is awesome; this is the only way I can describe it. I think the gift of faith is different from the measure of faith that God has given to all of us. We cannot control the gift of faith—only the Holy Spirit can.

Sometimes this gift of faith is here for a moment and then gone. I have been amazed so many times, year after year, by this amazing gift. It often works with the word of knowledge or wisdom. It also works with the healing and miracle gifts.

I believe it is the gift of faith that we experience when we have that special moment of asking Jesus into our heart. Suddenly we know, because we know—Jesus loves me; my sins are forgiven. He is with me, and He is never going to leave me. It is not necessarily an emotional experience, but it is a confident assurance and it fills us with peace and joy.

Pauline and I have been blessed so many times to see the visible transformation in someone's face, when the Holy Spirit comes down on them and they are filled with faith. Someone would ask for prayer, for a healing or a miracle in their home or family, and as we prayed, suddenly they would change before our eyes. We could see the glory of God in their face; it would light up, and they would be filled with faith.

There were other times when people asked for prayer, but I did not have faith for their request. So I told them, "I do not have faith for that."

Their answer was, "That's okay. I have the faith. You just do the praying." I did, and they were healed!

Who is to understand these things? There were times when I could see someone needed a miracle or healing. I would tell them that I was going to pray for them. They would answer, "I don't believe in that!"

My answer was, "I don't care. I believe!" I laid my hands on them and prayed—and they were healed.

Sometimes a group of us would lay hands on a person for healing. Then someone would speak up and say, "This person is healed!" Suddenly the person being prayed over would become aware that they were healed and start praising God.

With some people, their faith has to be stirred up. This happens often with families and their children; the parents were worried about their children. Worry and faith are opposites. Where there is worry, faith is not being applied. I would ask these parents, "Do you believe God is at work in your children?"

Their answer would often be, "Yes!"

I would ask them again, "Do you really believe that?"

"Yes!" Suddenly their faith would rise up, and the fear and worry were gone—faith had replaced it. We could see the change in their countenances. I now realize faith is visible if you look for it.

Interestingly, there are different faiths in the world, and they each have a different look. The faith that comes from God, through Jesus Christ by the Holy Spirit, is filled with power and authority. It gives us peace in very trying times of our lives. It is filled with light and grace, and transforms people and sets them free.

23

Gifts of Healing & Miracles

... to another gifts of healing by the one Spirit, and to another the effecting of miracles, —1 Corinthians 12:9-10

I never considered the healing gifts until after I was baptized in the Holy Spirit. This was amazing to me, because I had gone to church off and on for many years. I must have been deaf or else they never talked about the healing gifts in church.

I did hear about miracles and healings taking place in special places, so I believed in them. But I never heard anyone in my church speak of having received one. I never realized that they could happen to me or through me—that healing was for the whole church.

I got a hunger for the Bible so I bought one and started reading it. When I got to Mark 16:17-18, I read:

"And these signs will accompany those who have believed: in My name they will cast out demons; they will speak with new tongues; they will pick up serpents, and if they drink any deadly poison, it will not hurt them; they will lay hands on the sick, and they will recover."

As read "they will lay hands on the sick and they will recover" the Holy Spirit stopped me. I read it over and over. I said, "Lord, you are telling me that I can lay hands on the sick and they will recover."

Then I asked the Lord this question: "Lord, we have several churches in town; why don't I see or hear about any of this happening?"

He answered, "No one has faith enough to do it!"

I replied, "All right, I am going to try it and see if it works!"

To my surprise I found it did work and that there is healing in the hands of the church. It has been there from the time Christ walked on this earth.

Jesus said that signs shall follow those who have believed. What is it that we are to believe? We must believe that by His stripes we are healed. We must believe in Jesus Christ. And just as important, we must believe there is healing in our hands.

I often ask people to look at their hands, and I ask them, "Do you believe there is healing in your hands?"

Many will say, "Yes."

I then ask, "Do you give it away?"

Some will say, "I don't know how to pray."

And I say, "That is okay. You don't have to know how to pray. All you have to do is act and lay your hands on someone for healing. It doesn't have to be a big show. You can be in a hospital room with other people; they don't even have to be aware of what you are doing. Just reach out and lay your hand or hands on the person and believe that healing is flowing into their body. You can continue right on with your conversations—just believe and act."

There is also the healing ministry and the gifts of healing. In the healing ministry, the Holy Spirit chooses to use certain people and He anoints them for this purpose. They lay hands on people, anoint them with oil, and pray over them, and many people are healed through these ministries.

Other times, the Holy Spirit will have some individual go and touch someone in a church, a group, or a home, and that special gift of healing happens and the person is healed.

The healing gift is for all of us. When we as an individual need healing, there are things we need to do, but it seems as if many people are unaware of this and do not do what the Bible says:

> *Is anyone among you sick? Let him call for the elders of the church, and let them pray over him, anointing him with oil in the name of the Lord; and the prayer offered in faith will restore the one who is sick, and the Lord will raise him up, and if he has committed sins, they will be forgiven him. (James 5:14-15)*

It surprises me that so few people will act on these Scriptures. I don't know if it is a lack of teaching, or if it is because we have too much pride to ask our priests, pastors, or deacons or our Christian group to come and pray for us.

Our priest in Barton opened the Sunday service one morning by saying, "We will have prayer for anyone who needs healing; just come forward." The church was full of people, but Pauline was the only one who went up for prayer and she was healed on the spot. I cannot believe she was the only sick person in the church that day. Some folks travel all over the world looking for healing, but they will not go to their own church and pastors and ask for it.

Pauline and I have laid hands on many people for healing. Sometimes we see immediate healing, and sometimes it is a slow process. Some folks say, "I laid my hands for healing and nothing happened!"

I decided a long time ago that if one person in every hundred is healed, I would keep doing it just the same. I believe every time we lay hands on someone and pray for them, something happens—whether we see it or not. There is healing in our hands!

You must remember what Jesus said: "I only do what my Father tells me to do." I pray every morning for the wisdom and knowledge from God, so when we are asked to visit someone in the hospital or home we will know what to say and do to be a blessing. It is very important to be sensitive to the guidance and direction of the Holy Spirit and do what the Father wants done.

But there are times when He says nothing. I go just the same because the Scriptures tell us to lay hands on one another for healing. Other times, He will give me clear direction of what to say and do. When I obey Him, wonderful things happen.

The Holy Spirit has taught me so much from the Bible. You have maybe noticed I often say, "The Holy Spirit told me this" or "the Holy Spirit showed me that." The Holy Spirit has been my primary teacher for many years.

Jesus did so many wonderful healings. As I read about them in the Gospels, the Holy Spirit showed me that many times Jesus did not need to heal them; instead He set them free from a spirit of infirmity. He took authority over a spirit and commanded it to leave, and the person was well.

I often wondered why in some cases I could lay hands on a sick person over and over and have no results. Some of these were heart problems, skin problems, arthritic and nerve problems, and many other things the doctors were unable to find an answer to.

Now I know the reason for this: some of these things were spiritual things. The root of it was not in the flesh, mind, or soul, but in the spirit of the person. Medicine and drugs will not solve this type of problem. Laying on of hands will not solve this problem. The only way to deal with this type of sickness is to take authority over the spirit, bind it, and command it to leave. As a rule, in a day or two all the symptoms will be gone. We have seen this happen many times.

There is a root to all our sicknesses and diseases. The root can be in the flesh, our physical body; it can be in our soul, our mind or emotions; or it can be in our spirit. But the root must be dealt with if the person wants to be free from the sickness or disease.

I know some afflictions start with our emotions, such as fear. I believe some cancers start from a fear of cancer. We have had so many people come to us for prayer, because they are afraid of cancer, afraid of losing their sight, afraid they will become a cripple.

Another root is guilt. Some people believe they should be punished; the sickness they have is their punishment, and they deserve to be sick.

Other people want to be weak and sick, because it brings them attention. If they were healthy, they think no one would pay them any attention.

I have learned one thing about praying for sickness and infirmities: we must ask God to give us the wisdom and knowledge of the root problem and how to pray or deal with it.

When Pauline and I started to minister healing through the laying on of hands, I had a problem at first. Whenever I saw someone in a wheelchair, someone blind or deaf, or someone with cancer or some other serious problem, I felt that I did not have faith enough for those types of things.

I prayed about this problem, and the Lord showed me a truth that set me free from the fear, and now I can lay my hands and pray with faith for any problem. He showed me a vision of multitudes of people standing before Him. Then He asked me a question: "Do you see any wheelchairs or crippled people, anyone who is blind or deaf, or anyone with cancer or other disease here?"

I replied, "No Lord!"

He then said, "Everyone is totally healed and free. This is the way you need to see them, and you will not have a problem laying hands or praying for anyone, no matter how serious their affliction is." Since then, I have not had a problem laying hands on anyone for healing.

Sometimes we could not go and lay our hands in person on people for healing, so I would pray for them over the phone. I would have the person or someone who was with them lay their hands on them, and I would pray for God to heal them. There are so many ways God will heal, if we will only believe, act, and do something!

I could write this whole book on the miracles and healings we have seen, in our home, on the streets, in meetings, in the churches—healings of all kinds. Healing is not only for the body; it is for the mind, the soul, and the spirit too. The healing in our hands is for all these things.

It is so obvious there is healing in our hands. It should be pointed out to us as children. Have you ever had a hurt child run up to you, and you placed your hands on them and held them for a few moments, and then they ran off and started playing? There was healing in your hands!

Have you ever gone to someone who'd just lost a loved one? You didn't even know what to say, but you held their hands or just held them. Healing was happening. The heart and soul were being touched and comforted. I am sure this has happened to all of you many times.

I encourage you to use these wonderful gifts from God to the fullest in every opportunity you have each day.

24

The Gift of Tongues

... to another various kinds of tongues.—1 Corinthians 12:10

There is more controversy over tongues than any of the other gifts. Apparently Paul ran into this same problem too. He spent more time trying to explain the gift of tongues than he did any of the other gifts.

We need every spiritual gift God has given us. We have a problem with tongues, because the natural mind thinks it is foolish and cannot understand it, since tongues is a spiritual gift.

> *For one who speaks in a tongue does not speak to men, but to God; for no one understands, but in his spirit he speaks mysteries. But one who prophesies speaks to men for edification and exhortation and consolation. One who speaks in a tongue edifies himself; but one who prophesies edifies the church. (1 Corinthians 14:2-4.)*

Tongues is referred to as the least of the gifts, because it is the one gift that is for the individual. All the other gifts are for the other people. Notice what Paul said: it edifies the individual.

From what we have seen in forty years of ministry, many people in the church, including pastors, priests and ministers, need to be edified. It is very possible that many pastors and ministers get burned out because they lack the gift of tongues.

The gift of tongues is the most difficult gift for us to believe in because the natural mind has a problem with it. The gift of tongues functions from the spirit, not the mind. It is a mystery, and it is our spirit communicating with God. It is a very important gift to us as individuals.

This is what Paul said about it:

> *I thank God, I speak in tongues more than you all; however, in the church I desire to speak five words with my mind, that I may instruct*

others also, rather than ten thousand words in a tongue. (1 Corinthians 14:18-19)

Why would Paul say, "I speak in tongues more than you all?"

Because it edified him; it built him up spiritually for the work of the ministry. The word "edify" means to instruct or enlighten so as to encourage intellectual, moral, or spiritual improvement.

Every one of the gifts of the Holy Spirit is special. We should be very careful that we do not speak about them in such a way that people are frightened of them or have no desire to receive them. We do not want to put any of the gifts in a box or store them in a closet.

Our theologies and doctrines are not big enough to hold them; our natural mind is not large enough to hold them or understand them. We must use faith and function as spiritual men and women to learn and use the gifts of the Holy Spirit.

There are tongues that foreigners can understand. There are tongues that are for praise and worship. There are tongues for praying over someone when you don't know how to pray. There are other tongues that come with great authority and demons flee at the sound of them.

There are also messages in tongues for the church groups that need interpretation. Other times a message is for one individual and only that person understands it.

Now I wish that you all spoke in tongues, but even more that you would prophesy; and greater is one who prophesies than one who speaks in tongues, unless he interprets, so that the church may receive edifying. (1 Corinthians 14:5)

Why did Paul say, "I wish you all spoke in tongues?"

Paul knew that we all had the ability, that God did not give any of us a dumb spirit.

Many people do not use this ability for several reasons. Some have been taught from the time they were children that tongues is from the devil, but my Bible tells me it is a gift of the Holy

Spirit. Some are afraid of tongues, because they don't understand it. Others do not believe they have the ability.

There are others who do not believe in any of the gifts of the Holy Spirit. They have been taught by either their pastor or their church that these gifts are not valid anymore and the church does not need them. All we have to do is look around us to realize the church needs every gift of the Holy Spirit today.

The most important thing is that we are baptized in the Holy Spirit. When we are baptized in the Holy Spirit, every gift of the Holy Spirit is available in us. The Holy Spirit will use whoever is available and open. He is not like some teachers who have their favorite students—the Holy Spirit is not a respecter of persons. Through these years of ministry every one of the gifts has been manifested through Pauline and me.

I know that there are a variety of ministries—teaching, prayer, healing and so forth. But I also know that most ministries, to be effective, require the manifesting of several gifts, not only one gift each.

Paul did such a wonderful job of teaching about tongues in 1 Corinthians 14:14-15:

> *For if I pray in a tongue, my spirit prays, but my mind is unfruitful. What is the outcome then? I shall pray with the spirit and I shall pray with the mind also; I shall sing with the spirit and I shall sing with the mind also.*

I would encourage any of you who do not understand tongues and its purpose, or have a problem with it, to pray, "Lord, help me to understand." Then read 1 Corinthians 14 several times and let the Holy Spirit show you clearly the balance Paul wanted us to have. The gifts of the Holy Spirit are the tools of the Christian worker!

25

Gifts of Prophecy, Discernment, Interpretation

... to another prophecy, and to another the distinguishing of spirits ..., and to another the interpretation of tongues. —1 Corinthians 12:10

I found this group—prophecy, distinguishing of spirits, interpretation of tongues—are very similar in some ways. They all need proper discernment; they need interpretation. This is because they do not function through the natural mind, so it must grab on to them and bring them into our natural memory.

I have always tried to encourage Christian people in the use of the gifts of the Spirit. I think they are very important and are needed in the church. However, I also recognize the need to distinguish spirits and test the interpretation given tongues, because other spirits are prophesying and the tongues are not always interpreted correctly, misleading people who are anxious for a word from God.

Be aware that there are many prophets in the world today. Many are false prophets, and some of them are in the Christian church. If a person is called to be a pastor, a miracle worker, an interpreter, or a prophet they do not have to go around shouting it. Over a period of time these offices or positions become very obvious. God has His own way of confirming these ministries.

One thing we should all pray for is good discernment. Webster's dictionary defines discernment this way: "The quality of being able to grasp and comprehend what is obscure." To discern means to separate, to distinguish between, to detect with other senses than the vision.

I like this dictionary definition of discernment: "to grasp and comprehend what is obscure." When do we need to be discerning? All the time!

In this Scripture, notice that discernment goes with maturity and with training:

But solid food is for the mature, who because of practice have their senses trained to discern good and evil. (Hebrews 5:14)

To have good discernment our senses need to be trained. What senses? Our spiritual senses as well as our natural senses.

Several years ago, a woman told me they were leaving and going out to the Midwest and named the city they were going to. She asked me if I knew of a church there that was really alive; they did not want to land up in a dead church. I asked her if she could tell the difference between life and death. She said, "Yes!"

I said, "Fine. Just go to a church and, if there is life there, stay. If it is dead, go to another one."

An interesting Scripture reading in 2 Corinthians 2:15-16 says,

For we are a fragrance of Christ to God among those who are being saved and among those who are perishing; to the one an aroma from death to death, to the other an aroma from life to life. And who is adequate for these things?

Have you ever been in a situation and you did not feel right? You felt unsettled in your soul and spirit. You were very uncomfortable with the conversation and the surroundings. Something was telling you that things weren't right there—you were experiencing discernment.

Discernment is an ability, both natural and spiritual, which works through our senses. The more we use them, the more discerning we become. It is a wonderful ability; we can use it in both the natural world and the spiritual world.

Have you ever noticed that people give off vibrations? I simply call them vibes. The previous Scripture called it an aroma. These vibes or aroma go out and touch the people around us. They can be angry vibes. They can be loving vibes. They also can be lying, deceiving vibes. These vibes are coming at you from the people around you, and you also are sending out vibes.

These vibes can be from the body, soul or spirit. When they come from the body, some people call it body language. It is up to us to discern which vibes are good and which vibes are bad. The good ones we receive; the bad ones we reject. When we begin to do this, we are discerning good and evil.

We also need to use discernment right within ourselves. We are to weigh and test our thoughts, discerning which thoughts are good and which are evil. We need to use discernment with our emotions and our imaginations too. They also can be good or evil.

Both our mind and our emotions send off vibes. As we learn to discern the thoughts and emotions, we can be in control of the vibes we send out.

As our discernment improves within us, we become aware of the spiritual world around us. We can begin to recognize other spirits who are in this world with us; some are good and some are evil. The angels and demons are both spiritual beings; some are sent to help us, others to trouble us.

Discernment is needed in all of the ministries in the church. In the healing ministry, many of the sicknesses and diseases have a spiritual root, which must be dealt with. Where there is demonic possession, we must have discernment to recognize that it is demonic and what the spirit is. In the prophetic and teaching ministries, discernment is needed to recognize the truth from the lie.

How do we learn good discernment? By weighing and testing everything, including our thoughts and our emotions. Read the Bible and have a good knowledge of what it teaches. Weigh and test that which is coming from other people, including your pastor, priest or minister.

We can all make mistakes, so we don't want to condemn someone just because they made a mistake in their teaching or ministry. But we do not want to be taken in by other people's mistakes. The more knowledge and wisdom we have, the better we are able to discern.

Not all the thoughts that come into our minds are ours. Some of those thoughts are God's thoughts, some are right from the enemy, and some we receive from the people around us. Our responsibility is to separate and distinguish between them, in order to discern these thoughts properly.

> *For who among men knows the thoughts of a man except the spirit of the man, which is in him? Even so the thoughts of God no one knows except the Spirit of God.*
> *Now we have received, not the spirit of the world, but the Spirit who is from God, that we might know the things freely given to us by God. (1 Corinthians 2:11-12)*

The natural mind cannot discern things properly. The spiritual man in you must do the discerning. Your spiritual man can distinguish which thoughts come from God, which come from you, and which come from the enemy or other sources.

> *But a natural man does not accept the things of the Spirit of God; for they are foolishness to him, and he cannot understand them, because they are spiritually appraised. But he who is spiritual appraises all things, yet he himself is appraised by no man. (1 Corinthians 2:14-15)*

As a natural man, we are not even able to judge the motives of our own heart, say nothing of judging someone else's motives. I have asked many people, "Do you know the difference between your soul and your spirit?"

Many answered, "I thought they were the same thing!"

No! The soul and spirit are two different things, just as the heart and lungs are two different organs in the same body. The soul gives us the ability to function in the natural world; the spirit gives us the ability to function in the spiritual realm.

> *For the word of God is living and active and sharper than any two-edged sword, and piercing as far as the division of soul and spirit, of both joints and marrow, and able to judge the thoughts and inten-*

tions of the heart. (Hebrews 4:12)

We need to be able to recognize which part of our being—body, soul or spirit— is controlling us. Is it the physical desire? Is it our emotions? Is it our mind? Or is it our spirit? I expect that all four are in control at one time or another, depending on the need of the moment.

I have been sitting here for a while, and my body is telling me that I need to get up and move around a little. Later, when I am in the store, I see a nice fishing pole, and I consider buying it. That is my desire. Then I get a nudge to pray for somebody's need. That is my spirit or the Holy Spirit.

> *For those who are according to the flesh set their minds on the things of the flesh, but those who are according to the Spirit, the things of the Spirit. For the mind set on the flesh is death, but the mind set on the Spirit is life and peace, because the mind set on the flesh is hostile toward God; for it does not subject itself to the law of God, for it is not even able to do so; and those who are in the flesh cannot please God. (Romans 8:5-8)*

Many people argue with God over this and say, "I can do it. My mind is good. I know right from wrong. I know the motives of my heart."

What we need to know is that our natural mind does not have the ability to understand or interpret spiritual things; only our spirit has the ability to do this. Our spiritual life is the highest part of our being, and it can do a good job of leading our body, soul and emotions if we allow it to.

But our soul does not want to relinquish control to our spirit. Our emotions demand to be expressed. Our physical body demands to have its way. We have a war going on inside of us, and only when we see that our spirit must be the controlling factor do we come to a place of peace and the war ends.

> *For if you are living according to the flesh, you must die; but if by the Spirit you are putting to death the deeds of the body, you will live. For all who are being led by the Spirit of God, these are sons of God. (Romans 8:13-14)*

As long as we continue allowing our natural mind or the desires of our flesh to lead us, we will constantly have serious problems in life. We need to practice discernment with our thinking and emotions.

Why do I need to practice discernment with my emotions? Because a lot of what you are feeling emotionally and stirring you up is not coming from your emotions; it is coming from some other source, perhaps other people or from God.

But it can be coming right from the pit, from some other spirit. When someone is filled with hate and anger, and you do not guard yourself, it touches you and you begin to feel the hatred and anger. You must recognize what is happening and block it.

When you feel God's love and peace, it is not yours. It is God's, but you are feeling it. You can embrace it and accept it and be blessed by it.

All these things and many more need good discernment. As we exercise this ability, it increases, and as a result we have a lot more peace and stability in our lives and in our homes.

Properly interpreting the gifts

We need to be able to interpret many gifts from God: dreams and visions, prophecy, the Bible, tongues, the words of wisdom and knowledge. To begin, we must realize these are all spiritual things. Since this is indeed the case, we need to approach them as spiritual men and women, not as natural people. We also must also recognize that some people are gifted by God in these different areas and look to them for help.

When it comes to dreams and visions, most of them are personal in nature. If they are personal, they need to be interpreted as such. Prophecy and tongues can also be for the individual; if so they must be recognized as such and kept personal.

One of the difficulties with the gifts of the Holy Spirit that I have seen is in the area of correction. People are afraid to correct someone if they recognize the person is not using the gift properly or if they are in the wrong spirit when ministering it. The Scripture tells us to test every spirit.

I have heard a lot of prophesies and tongues that came from the person themselves, not from God. Some of them were harmless, but some were very misleading, directing individuals and churches into a ministry that the Holy Spirit had nothing to do with.

When we are dealing with these gifts that need interpretation, we also need confirmation from other sources such as the anointing of the Holy Spirit or the living Word speaking to us in other ways. The Lord doesn't mind speaking to us more than once.

26

My God Is Big

The Lord wants us to increase and become much larger in many areas of our lives. None of us are fully aware of the capabilities we have as children of God. Our thinking is small, and our awareness of who we are in Jesus Christ is limited.

I think of a book I read years ago, "Mr. God, This is Anna." This was a small book filled with big thoughts. A young man had found this little girl on the streets and he brought her home and his family cared for her. She had a very simple, but very profound relationship with God. She would talk to God and say, "Mr. God, this is Anna." If you can find the book, get it and read it.

They started sending this little girl to Sunday school. After three or four times, she wouldn't go anymore. They asked her why. She answered, "The teacher is afraid and she is making God small."

My question is: do you have a big God or a small God? I expect if our God is small, we are small as well.

When I started to read the Bible, the Holy Spirit would not allow me to read any of the comments from the bottom of the pages or the other commentaries that were available. Later I realized why—He did not want me to become bound by other people's thinking.

He was able to make me see some things I would not have seen if I had read those commentaries. I am not saying the commentaries are wrong. They are a great help, but they can, and do, affect how we interpret the Scriptures.

One of the things I saw clearly was that the Lord was constantly doing things differently. I had been told by some folks that if you can't find it in the Bible, it is not from God. This is not the truth; if you believe it, you are making God small.

Jesus did not do the same things over and over. He was always doing things in a different way, not being repetitious. The Bible shows us that God was always doing something different. The Bible itself tells us it would take many books to contain all the things which God has said or done.

Repetition can happen so quickly in ministry. We pray or do something in a certain way and it works. Then we want to do the same thing over and over—even when it no longer works. It has become a dead work. We no longer need the Holy Spirit; we can do it ourselves.

Concerning the gifts of the Holy Spirit, I ask: are they large or small? It depends on the person and their faith. I believe there is no limit as to how large the gifts of the Holy Spirit are; it is our faith that limits them.

> *Now to Him who is able to do far more exceeding abundantly beyond all that we ask or think, according to the power that works within us. (Ephesians 3:20)*

I had a vision several years ago. There was a very large field, and it was full of little boxes. I could see there was a person in every box. Then I saw a large finger come down from above and break open one of the boxes. A person came running out, put the box back together, and rushed back inside.

I said, "Lord, what are you showing me?"

He replied: "I am setting my people free, but they go right back into their bondage. I want them to live outside of their boxes, but they are afraid of freedom and of the responsibility that goes with it!"

What about your thinking, is it large or small? With Jesus and the Holy Spirit, we are capable of so many things. I think our capabilities should be increasing. We should be seeing new possibilities day after day, as God increases us.

Can we look ahead and say, "God has some big things in my future?" If I only take what I have right now and use it to the fullest, there is going to be an increase.

For it is just like a man about to go on a journey, who called his own slaves, and entrusted his possessions to them. And to one he gave five talents, to another, two, and to another, one, each according to his own ability; and he went on his journey.

Immediately the one who had received the five talents went and traded with them, and gained five more talents. In the same manner the one who had received the two talents gained two more. But he who received the one talent went away, and dug in the ground, and hid his master's money.

Now after a long time the master of those slaves came and settled accounts with them. And the one who had received the five talents came up and brought five more talents, saying," Master, you entrusted five talents to me; see, I have gained five more talents."

His master said to him, "Well done, good and faithful slave; you were faithful with a few things, I will put you in charge of many things, enter into the joy of your master."

The one also who had received the two talents came up and said, "Master, you entrusted two talents to me; see, I have gained two more talents."

His master said to him, "Well done, good and faithful slave; you were faithful with a few things, I will put you in charge of many things; enter into the joy of your master."

And the one also who had received the one talent came up and said, "Master, I knew you to be a hard man, reaping where you did not sow, and gathering where you scattered no seed. And I was afraid, and went away and hid your talent in the ground; see, you have what is yours."

But his master answered and said to him, "You wicked, lazy slave, you knew that I reap where I did not sow and gather where I scattered no seed. Then you ought to have put my money in the bank, and on my arrival I would have received my money back with interest. Therefore take away the talent from him, and give it to the one who has the ten talents."

For to everyone who has, more shall be given, and he shall have an abundance; but from the one who does not have, even what he does have shall be taken away. And cast out the worthless slave into the outer darkness; in that place there will be weeping and gnashing of teeth. (Matthew 25:14-30)

God is big! He is out to make you and me big. What is it that makes us big? Getting out of our boxes! As long as I can think only of myself, my problems, my difficulties, my pain and poor little me, I remain small. When I can get out of myself, begin to see others have it so much more difficult than me, and do everything I can to help them, I get bigger.

Remember the parable about the Good Samaritan and the priest and Levite? The Good Samaritan was big; the other two were small.

Jesus said, "You will do all the things I have done and more!" In order to do this, we must allow the Holy Spirit to become active in our lives, get outside of ourselves, and start using our talents and gifts the Holy Spirit gives us so freely.

We have a big God. Jesus was big. He wants us to be big also.

Part Three

The Spiritual Foundation

27

The Only Foundation

"Therefore everyone who hears these words of Mine, and acts upon them, may be compared to a wise man, who built his house upon the rock. And the rain descended, and the floods came, and the winds blew, and burst against that house; and yet it did not fall, for it had been founded upon the rock.

"And everyone who hears these words of Mine, and does not act upon them, will be like a foolish man, who built his house upon the sand. And the rain descended, and the floods came, and the winds blew, and burst against that house; and it fell, and great was its fall."— Matthew 7:24-27

We can build a house with no foundation; it can be a very good looking house. Or we can build a house on a bad or weak foundation, but it can be a good looking house too. In our spiritual walk, our foundation or lack of foundation is referring to what we believe, what it is that we have faith in.

For no man can lay a foundation other than the one which is laid, which is Jesus Christ. (1 Corinthians 3:11)

This Scripture is telling us that we don't need to build a foundation; there is one already laid. That is the one we need to build our spiritual house on. Jesus spoke in John 5: 39-40:

"You search the Scriptures, because you think that in them you have eternal life; and it is these that bear witness of Me; and you are unwilling to come to Me, that you may have life."

Does your faith waver every time it is put to the test?
Do you sink into depression with every storm that comes your way?
Do you fall with every temptation?
Do you walk in the flesh more than in the spirit?

Do you always need others praying for you and encouraging you?

Can you stand firm against the spiritual attacks of the enemy?

If these problems and others always seem to be bothering you, look to your foundation, for this is where the problem lies.

Many of us rely upon the church that we go to as our foundation. Others rely on their rituals and traditions. Still others use the Bible as their foundation, saying, "I stand on the Scriptures!"

Some put their trust in a person—a priest or pastor, a nun or saint, or Mary, the mother of Jesus. Some folks put their trust in their own goodness and the good works they do for others and the church. There is a place for these things in our spiritual walk, but they are not to be our foundation. The Scriptures are very clear. There is only one foundation that individuals can lay for their salvation and entry into the kingdom of God: it is a person, Jesus Christ.

The question everyone in the world has to answer is this: no matter how good you are or what religion you practice, was Jesus telling the truth? Was Jesus lying when He said that He is the only way to the Father?

> *Jesus said to him, "I am the way, and the truth, and the life; no one comes to the Father but through Me." (John 14:6)*

> *Jesus answered him, "If I do not wash you, you have no part with Me." (John 13:8)*

Jesus said some pretty provocative things. In Matthew 7:13-14, He said:

> *"Enter by the narrow gate; for the gate is wide, and the way is broad that leads to destruction, and many are those who enter by it. For the gate is small, and the way is narrow that leads to life, and few are those that find it."*

If these things are true, then we need to pay heed to them. Our life depends on it.

What Jesus is saying to me is this: "You have to start with Me; there is no other place to start."

Why is it that we have to start with Jesus? Because our heart has to be changed and our sins have to be washed away; only Jesus Christ can do this!

> *And I shall give them one heart, and shall put a new spirit within them. And I shall take the heart of stone out of their flesh and give them a heart of flesh,, that they may walk in My statutes and keep My ordinances, and do them. Then they will be My people, and I will be their God. (Ezekiel 11:19-20)*

As I look back to my younger years I can see what one of my major problems was: I had a heart of stone. No wonder my life was such a mess, and my marriage was falling apart!

We can join a church and not receive a new heart. We can grow up in church and not receive a new heart. We can be a good Baptist, Catholic, or Pentecostal and not have a new heart. Our church cannot give us a new heart; only God can.

We receive a new heart when we go to God, have an authentic conversion experience and are born again of the Spirit. The church is not the foundation! It is Jesus Christ who is the foundation that the church is built on. There is no foundation that any man can lay other than Jesus Christ.

28

Foundation Building Blocks

Therefore leaving the elementary teaching about the Christ, let us press on to maturity, not laying again a foundation of repentance from dead works and of faith toward God, of instruction about washings, and laying on of hands, and the resurrection of the dead, and eternal judgment.—Hebrews 6:1-2

If we want a solid foundation, there are a number of steps the Bible identifies we must take. First is calling on or receiving Jesus Christ as our Lord and Savior. Next we must lay the necessary building blocks for us to have a strong spiritual foundation.

Looking at Hebrews 6:1-2, we can see six building blocks that we need. Note that Christ is involved in every one of them:

1. Repentance from dead works: Jesus brings a change of direction in our life.
2. Faith toward God: Jesus is the author and finisher of our faith.
3. Instructions about washings: baptism of water; we join Jesus in His death. Baptism of the Holy Spirit; Jesus is the baptizer.
4. Laying on of hands: the life of Jesus flows through us for blessing, healing, gifts and ministry.
5. Resurrection of the dead: Jesus is the resurrection and the life; we join Him in His resurrection.
6. Eternal judgment: Jesus is the Lamb of God who died for our sins.

And I saw between the throne and the elders a Lamb standing, as if slain. (Revelation 5:6)

For the Lamb in the center of the throne shall be their Shepherd, and shall guide them to springs of the water of life. (Revelation 7:17)

According to the grace of God that was given to me, as a wise master builder I laid a foundation, and another is building upon it. But let each man be careful how he builds upon it; for no man can lay a foundation other then the one which is laid, which is Christ Jesus. (1 Corinthians 3:10-11)

The commission that Paul received from Jesus was "to open their eyes so that they might turn from darkness to light" (Acts 26:18). Many religious, law abiding people lived in darkness; their foundation was religious practices and keeping the law. Paul spent much of his time trying to free people from the bondages of religion and law and bring them into a relationship with Jesus Christ and the Holy Spirit.

In one place, Paul said, "Follow me!"

Paul had received abundant revelation from God. Through this revelation, Paul saw the difference between law and grace. He saw that the law was unable to change him or anyone else, but that the grace of God through Jesus Christ and the Holy Spirit could transform us. Paul made this very clear in his letter to the Galatians:

You foolish Galatians, who has bewitched you, before whose eyes Jesus Christ was publicly portrayed as crucified? This is the only thing I want to find out from you: did you receive the Spirit by the works of the Law, or by hearing with faith? Are you so foolish? Having begun by the Spirit, are you now being perfected by the flesh? (Galatians 3:1-3)

Paul spoke of the same problem again in very blunt terms that we should all be able to understand:

You have been severed from Christ, you who are seeking to be justified by law; you have fallen from grace. (Galatians 5:4)

Some churches today are preaching law instead of grace. Some of these churches that have the reputation of being alive are really dead, even as the church of Sardis in the book of Revelation.

In the past several years there has been a large increase in the church. Many have come to know the Lord Jesus Christ as their personal Savior. They have been baptized with water and the Holy Spirit, and they began a spiritual journey. But now, after five or ten years, many of them have already fallen into the trap of the foolish Galatians—they are trying to perfect themselves by the law.

29

Building Block #1 Repentance From Dead Works

... not laying again a foundation of repentance from dead works— Hebrews 6:1

The word "repentance" means a change of direction. It also means to feel contrite or sorry—sorry enough that we do make a change. It can also mean a change of action, a change of thought or a change of heart. In Christian use, repentance would mean turning away from sin and turning to God. The parable of the prodigal son is a beautiful example of repentance.

Dead works are things that do not produce life for you. They are all those things you are trying to do to manipulate God, things in which you are trying to get His approval, things you are doing in trying to pay your own way into the kingdom of God.

Not all repentance is pleasing or acceptable to God. We can see this in the parable about the two men who went up to the temple to pray, one a Pharisee, and the other a tax-gatherer. One was very proud, the other very humble.

It is very easy for us to look around and think, "I am glad I am not like that person. I know the Lord, I am filled with the Holy Spirit, and I am doing good things for God." We can do all these things, yet have very little change inside our heart.

Then you might think, "What hope is there for me? I have tried and I don't seem to be getting any victories." Paul must have felt the same way when he said:

Wretched man that I am! Who will set me free from the body of this death? Thanks be to God through Jesus Christ our Lord! (Romans 7:24-25).

King David also understood that God had something to do

with our repenting and changing our ways. He was aware that he could not change himself, but God could change him if he allowed Him to. In Psalms 51:1-2, he prayed:

> *Be gracious to me, O God, according to Thy loving kindness; according to the greatness of Thy compassion blot out my transgressions. Wash me thoroughly from my iniquity, and cleanse me from my sin.*

Then in Psalms 51:10, he prayed:

> *Create in me a clean heart, O God, and renew a steadfast spirit within me*

I believe that our first act of repentance is the cry from our heart: "God I want to be different; I don't like what I am and the things I do. God help me!"

> *Or do you think lightly of the riches of His kindness and forbearance and patience, not knowing that the kindness of God leads you to repentance? (Romans 2:4)*

God said He would take the stony heart from us and give us a clean heart, a heart of flesh. This is where we have to start. We cannot repent until we can see that we need to change. The Ten Commandments are not there for us to live by; they are there so we can see that we need to change. This is their major purpose!

The act of repentance is not just a one moment decision. It is ongoing, day by day, made up of many decisions to do right or wrong, to serve God or to serve myself.

30

Building Block #2 Faith Toward God

... and of faith toward God—Hebrews 6:1

I ask you the question, what or who do you have faith in? Most of you would answer, "In God, of course!" But we need to give the question more thought than just a quick answer, if we want faith to be one of our foundational building blocks.

What if you could go back and ask God's people wandering around in the desert the same question? I wonder what their answer would be. They wandered around in the desert for forty years and then they died there, because of their lack of faith. Maybe we can't get out of our own private deserts for the same reason.

There is a difference between *faith* and *belief*. We can believe in God and yet not have faith in God or trust Him. I would define the two words like this: *belief* is the mental acceptance of something as true; *faith* is the complete acceptance of something not accepted by reason.

There always seems to be quite a lot of controversy in the church over the strong faith ministries. A book came out a while back titled, "Faith or Presumption." This is another way of asking if it is faith or a mistaken or assumed belief.

Faith and belief do not come from the same source. Faith is a gift of God that comes from the heart or spirit. Belief comes from the mind and reasoning of man. If I rephrase my question, "Do you believe in God or do you have faith in God?" what would your answer be?

If you look to your mind, you would find what you believe. But if you look to your heart and spirit, you would know what you have faith for. Many people believe in God, but not all have faith in God.

This building block is the kind of faith that the writer of Hebrews 11:1 speaks of:

> *Now faith is the assurance of things hoped for, the conviction of things not seen.*

I have heard this statement a number of times: "Faith is blind!" Even the dictionary seems to imply that faith is blind, but this is not the truth.

Faith sees the unseen things that the natural eye cannot see. Faith shows us there is life after death, there are miracles, there is another dimension beyond the physical.

There are spiritual laws as well as physical laws, and the law of faith works when applied. Faith shows us the truth that the natural man is unable to see. The man who says, "There is no God!" is in total darkness, but he thinks he is in the light.

We can look at two men in the Bible: King Saul and King David. Which one of these men were men of faith? Which man do you think pleased God? King Saul believed in God alright, but King David had faith in God. It was King David who was pleasing to God.

Faith and hope are different. I have heard a lot of people say, "I hope so!" The next step for these people is to receive assurance that what they hoped for is going to happen. This is when faith has come. Then they can say, "I know, because I know. God has heard my prayer, and He is going to answer it!"

This is the faith that is a foundational building block. This is the faith that keeps me from sinking in the sand in every storm. This faith is in Jesus Christ and what He did for me on the cross. With this faith, I can go boldly to the throne of God in my time of need. This is the faith we direct toward Jesus Christ, the rock of our salvation, the only solid foundation there is for any of us.

31

Building Block #3
Instructions About Washings

... of instruction about washings—Hebrews 6:2

Some of the Bible versions use the word *baptism* instead of washings. Both of these words imply action, but more than action is involved: faith also must be involved. You will find faith must be applied in every one of the foundational building blocks. Without faith, they are meaningless activities.

For example when we go to take communion, we need to apply faith that something special is happening between God and us. In a marriage ceremony, we also apply faith that God is blessing this union in a special way. In praying, we apply faith that God is hearing our prayer.

There are two baptisms involved in the Christian spiritual foundation. One is the baptism of water, the other the baptism of the Holy Spirit. Both of these stir up a lot of controversy. Churches divide over these two issues. Should we baptize as babies or as adults? When should it be done and by whom? Should we be sprinkled or submerged?

This is also true with the baptism of the Holy Spirit. In some churches, it is called confirmation and done by a bishop. In other churches, the members lay hands on the believer for the manifestation of the Spirit, expecting people to pray in tongues as proof. And there are others who believe that when you are born again, you are filled with the Holy Spirit.

The Scriptures declares, "You will know them by their fruit." Both of these baptisms should be life-changing. The fruit we should see is the fruit of the Holy Spirit—peace, love, joy, faith and forgiveness. If the fruit of the Spirit does not appear in the person's life, I would doubt the validity of their conversion or confirmation. In both of these baptisms, we must apply faith to the action.

Why do I need to be baptized with water? Because it deals with our sin issue! The best teaching on the purpose of water baptism is in Romans 6:1-4. Paul says:

> *What shall we say then? Are we to continue in sin that grace might increase? May it never be! How shall we who died to sin still live in it? Or do you not know that all of us who have been baptized into Christ Jesus have been baptized into His death?*
> *Therefore we have been buried with Him through baptism into death, in order that as Christ was raised from the dead through the glory of the Father, so we to might walk in newness of life.*

When we ask Christ into our hearts, we receive eternal life! When we go through the water of baptism, we become united with Christ in His death on the cross.

Paul continues in Romans 6:6:

> *Knowing this, that our old self was crucified with Him, that our body of sin might be done away with, that we should no longer be slaves to sin.*

Once we have applied faith, gone through the waters of baptism, and joined Jesus in His death on the cross, we do not have any excuse to continue in sin, because the old sin nature is gone. We can continue to sin, but we don't have to; we are not slaves to sin any longer. We continue to sin because we like to and enjoy it!

If you read Romans 6 carefully, praying that you will understand it, you will see that water baptism is dealing with death—not only the death of Christ, but the death of our own sinful nature. Something very real and powerful happens in baptism, if we apply faith. It is more than just a testimony to the world that we have accepted Jesus Christ as our Savior.

We should have a funeral service at every baptism, celebrating the death and burial of our old sinful nature. Then the reality of the death of the sinful nature would be more real to us.

Do you believe that Jesus Christ died on the cross? Do you have faith that you died on the cross with Him? That is what we must believe, otherwise we have a weakness in our spiritual foundation. Not only do we believe we died with Him, we must believe we are buried with Him.

The following Scriptures are telling us that we must join Christ in His death and in His burial, if we are to join Him in His resurrection.

> *Therefore we have been buried with Him through baptism into death, in order that as Christ was raised from the dead through the glory of the Father, so we to might walk in newness of life. (Romans 6:4)*

> *Having been buried with Him in baptism, in which you were also raised up with Him through faith in the working of God, who raised Him from the dead. (Colossians 2:12)*

Another part of our spiritual foundation is the baptism of the Holy Spirit. Why is it important that I be baptized in the Holy Spirit? The following Scriptures make it very clear why we need the Holy Spirit:

> *"You shall receive power when the Holy Spirit has come upon you; and you shall be My witness both in Jerusalem, and in all of Judea and Samaria, and even to the remotest parts of the earth." (Acts 1:8)*

> *"And I will ask the Father, and He will give you another Helper, that He may be with you forever." (John 14:16)*

> *"But the Helper, the Holy Spirit, whom the Father will send in My name, He will teach you all things, and bring to your remembrance all that I said to you." (John 14:26)*

> *"When the Helper comes, whom I will send to you from the Father, that is the Spirit of truth, who proceeds from the Father, He will bear witness of Me." (John 15:26)*

> *"But when He, the Spirit of truth, comes, He will guide you into all the truth: for He will not speak on His own initiative, but whatever He hears, He will speak; and He will disclose to you what is to come. He shall glorify Me: for He shall take of Mine, and disclose it to you. All*

> *things that the Father has are Mine; therefore I said, that He takes of Mine, and will disclose it to you." (John 16:13-15)*

Christian people can be very gullible when it comes to other Christians, especially if they are in positions of leadership. We quickly believe lies, if they sound good and are coming from the proper people.

These lies have been taught to us from the time we were children by well-intentioned people who believed the lies themselves. One of the very important works of the Holy Spirit is to free you from the lies that you think are truth and to bring you into the real truth. Can we have a solid foundation for our lives based on lies? No! Only the truth can give us a solid foundation.

The best teachers we have in the church or in the world cannot take the place of the Holy Spirit in our lives. We cannot enter into a spiritual walk with Jesus Christ and our Father apart from the Holy Spirit. The work of the Holy Spirit is to lead us from the darkness into the light, to bring us into the fullness of who God created us to be.

32

Building Block #4
Laying on of Hands

... and laying on of hands—Hebrews 6:2

To some people laying on hands seems like plain foolishness. In fact, many of the things that come from God seem to be foolish—for instance, God sending His Son to die on the cross for our sins. But to those who have faith, laying on of hands is one of the ways God chooses to manifest His blessing, power and authority for healing, anointing, and baptizing in the Holy Spirit.

The question is: what purpose does the laying on of hands serve? The answer is in the Scriptures:

> *" ... they will lay hands on the sick, and they will recover." (Mark 16:18)*
>
> *Then, when they had fasted and prayed and laid their hands upon them, they sent them away. (Acts 13:3)*
>
> *And when Paul had laid his hands upon them, the Holy Spirit came on them, and they began speaking with tongues and prophesying. (Acts 19:6)*

In the Old Testament, blessing was bestowed by the laying on of hands. We can lay hands on our children when they are not feeling well. We can lay hands and bless them when we send them off to school. Husbands and wife can lay hands on one another and bless each other.

Faith is once again involved. Do I believe? Can I lay my hands on the sick for healing? Can I lay my hands on my children and send them off to school, believing God is going to help them and guard them? As a Christian, can I lay my hands on others for the baptism of the Holy Spirit?

However, it is not just a matter of us laying our hands on other folks, but of having others lay their hands on us for physical healing or for a blessing. Have you had other Christian folks lay hands on you for the baptism of the Holy Spirit or for the power and authority you need to do His work?

Jesus declared, "You will do the things I do and even more." This is a very important issue for all Christian people. Laying on of hands is a necessary act if we are to go forth in the world and do the things Jesus did. We will need His power and authority to do it.

33

Building Block #5
Resurrection of the Dead

... and the resurrection of the dead—Hebrews 6:2

Is resurrection an important issue? If you consider what the Bible says about our condition, it is vitally important. In Ephesians 2:1-6, it says:

> *And you were dead in your trespasses and sins, in which you formally walked according to the course of this world, according to the prince of the power of air, of the spirit that is now working in the sons of disobedience.*
> *Among them we too formally lived in the lusts of our flesh, indulging the desires of the flesh and of the mind, and were by nature children of wrath, even as the rest.*
> *But God, being rich in mercy, because of His great love with which He loved us, even when we were dead in our transgressions, made us alive together with Christ (by grace you have been saved), and raised us up with Him, and seated us with Him in the heavenly places, in Christ Jesus.*

Resurrection is a vital part of our foundation, because we are dead until we go to Jesus for life. In John 11:25, Jesus said to the woman,

> *"I am the resurrection and the life; he who believes in Me shall live even if he dies, and everyone who lives and believes in Me shall never die. Do you believe this?"*

You can't separate Jesus from resurrection, because without Jesus there is no resurrection. Without the cross and the death of Jesus, there is no entry through the veil into the Holy of Holies—to the throne of grace.

We all need resurrection, because of what God said in the

Garden of Eden: "but from the tree of the knowledge of good and evil you shall not eat, for in the day that you eat from it you shall surely die" (Genesis 2:17). When Adam and Eve ate from the fruit of the tree of knowledge of good and evil, we all died with them.

I expect most people reading Genesis 2:17 consider death to be a curse or a punishment from God. But it was not a curse! It was judgment against sin, against sickness in our physical bodies. Death brings an end to the sin and sickness. It brings liberation and freedom to the soul and spirit of man.

How would you like to live in that body of yours for 200 years as it gets old and sickly? How would you like to live in that old shell for a thousand years? I expect most would answer, "No, thanks!"

I have heard many elderly people say, "When are you coming to get me, Lord?" These folks are not afraid of death; they are alive and they know that death cannot touch them. These people have already been resurrected, and death will liberate their soul and spirit from a sick old body and they will go to the Lord.

34

Building Block #6 Eternal Judgment

... and eternal judgment—Hebrews 6:2

Many people live in guilt and fear. Some of us feel guilty because we *are* guilty. Where there is guilt, there is also fear.

One of the main reasons for fear is we believe that somewhere along the way we are going to be punished. The fear and guilt we live with seems to be a part of our punishment. We can be free of this feeling of condemnation, fear, and guilt by turning to Jesus Christ and receiving forgiveness of our sins.

Many people are afraid of death. One of the reasons is eternal judgment. What if I really am going to stand before God and be judged? We have all failed and fallen short. We have sinned against one another.

Wouldn't it be great if we could bring along a good lawyer to represent us? Afraid not! You are on your own unless you have someone to defend you, and there is only one who can do that: Jesus Christ.

When we are living in guilt and fear, it affects us in so many ways. It shows up in our speech and actions. It even shows up on our faces; it robs us of joy and takes the glow from our faces.

One of the Scriptures I have thought about every now and then says, "It's a terrible thing to fall into the hands of the living God." What this means to me is that God is relentless; when He gets a hold of you, He doesn't let go. He is not like us—kind of wishy-washy.

There is going to be a separating of the wheat and the tares! There is not going to be any room for excuses, because God has made Himself known to all people, even though some want to deny it.

> *"For God so loved the world, that He gave His only begotten Son, that whoever believes in Him should not perish, but have eternal life.*
> *For God did not send the Son into the world to judge the world, but that the world should be saved through Him.*
> *He who believes in Him is not judged; he who does not believe has been judged already, because he has not believed in the name of the only begotten Son of God." (John 3:16-18)*

It seems like God has placed the decision in our hands, whether or not we believe on the Lord Jesus Christ! The decision we make decides if we are the wheat or the tares.

> *My little children, I am writing these things to you that you may not sin. And if anyone sins, we have an advocate with the Father, Jesus Christ the righteous; and He Himself is the propitiation for our sins; and not for ours only, but also for those of the whole world. (1 John 2:1-2)*

> *" ... and He gave Him authority to execute judgment, because He is the Son of Man. Do not marvel at this; for an hour is coming, in which all who are in the tombs shall hear His voice, and shall come forth; those who did the good deeds to a resurrection of life, those who committed the evil deeds to a resurrection of judgment." (John 5:27-29)*

Jesus has laid a wonderful foundation for us. Now the question is how will we build on it?

> *So then, my beloved, just as you have always obeyed, not as in my presence only, but now much more in my absence, work out your salvation with fear and trembling; for it is God who is at work in you, both to will and to work for His good pleasure.*
> *Do all things without grumbling or disputing; that you may prove yourselves to be blameless and innocent, children of God above reproach in the midst of a crooked and perverse generation, among whom you appear as lights in the world. (Philippians 2:12-16)*

35

Stumbling Stones

The Bible is filled with warnings about the pitfalls, the stumbling stones in our spiritual journey. One of the books I read several times was "Pilgrim's Progress." If you have never read it, find one and read it. You will be able to relate to many of the pitfalls covered in this book.

We do have a spiritual enemy, and he is constantly trying to mislead us and bring our spiritual journey to a standstill. Satan doesn't care who you are, pastor, minister, priest, prayer leader, song leader or the person who sweeps out the church. If you have received Jesus as your Lord and Savior, Satan is going to place stumbling stones and pitfalls in your path to hinder you. He wants to rob you of your faith, joy, love, and peace.

Satan has been cast out of heaven, and he wants to keep you out of the kingdom of God as well. Satan is an expert at this; he has been around for a long time and knows every trick to defeat you.

One of the tools he uses is the law. He wants you to work very hard to be holy. St. Paul confronts this issue in Galatians 3:1-3:

> *You foolish Galatians, who has bewitched you, before whose eyes Jesus Christ was publicly portrayed as crucified? This is the only thing I want to find out from you: did you receive the Spirit by the works of the Law, or by hearing with faith? Are you so foolish? Having begun by the Spirit, are you now being perfected by the flesh?*

What happened to these foolish Galatians? Someone came along and brought them right back under the law. Notice the phrase, "did you receive the Spirit by the works of the Law, or by hearing with faith?" The works of the law are your own efforts to be holy and godly, instead of you accepting the righteousness that comes from Jesus and the cross. The only thing the works of law accomplishes is to cause you to become self-righteous—and that is sin.

You cannot receive the Holy Spirit by the works of the law! The only way you can receive the Holy Spirit is through Jesus Christ—it is freely given, just by believing.

Are you so foolish? Are you now trying to buy or earn a gift from God? Apparently the Galatians did not know that with all of their good works, they could not buy anything from God. There is not one of us who can pay the price for the smallest sin we have ever done!

Don't be fooled! The same thing is happening in our churches today. People are receiving the Lord in their hearts, being filled with the Holy Spirit, and going right back into their old patterns. They are not going anywhere spiritually. They are still trying to find favor with God and earn their way with good works. This is the exact pattern the foolish Galatians were following.

Some people have spent years studying the Bible, and they can recite large portions of it. The letter of the law has become their stumbling stone and they never understood the Spirit of the law. It all landed up in their head and never got to their heart.

Another way Satan works is to bring dissension in the church and in the family. I remember one church that needed a little more room for the children, so they decided to add another room for that purpose. But before they were finished, there was so much dissension the church split up over building this one little room.

In another family situation, where the man and wife both were Christians, the husband spent so much of his time at the church, doing all kinds of things. His wife tried to tell him that he needed to spend some time at home with his family, but he wouldn't listen to her, and they ended up separated.

There are times the enemy keeps us so busy doing Christian and church activity, that we have no time to serve God or our family.

People who are in ministries have the same problem. They start the ministry in service to God, but then over a period of time they are serving the ministry or their own inflated egos instead of God.

In Hebrews 5:11, it speaks of another hindrance:

Concerning Him we have much to say, and it is hard to explain, since you have become dull of hearing.

This is another hindrance that comes up over and over in the Old and New Testaments: "seeing they see not, and hearing they hear not."

Several years ago I was speaking in a church about learning to hear God's voice in a personal way. After the service, an elderly woman came up to me and said, "I am envious of you!" I asked her why she was envious of me.

She said, "Years ago I used to know God's voice, but I haven't heard Him for many years!" Had God stopped speaking to her? I don't think so. She had become dull of hearing.

Try this: on Monday go to all your church friends and ask them what the Sunday service message was. I am sure some of them will know, because they have learned to listen, but many others will have no idea.

Here is another question we should ask ourselves from time to time: where is my spiritual life going? Is it going anywhere? Am I backsliding? Am I at a standstill? Or am I going forward?

Because we go to church regularly, give money, read our Bible every day, sing in the choir, and pray every day, it does not mean we are growing spiritually. Remember, Paul was doing all these things, but he was at a standstill spiritually for years, until he met Jesus and began to walk with Him day by day.

Are you walking with Jesus day by day? Are you getting to know this Jesus in you, in a deeper more intimate way, as time goes on? This is the important issue; all these other things are not as important.

Thousands of times through the years, I have heard people

make this statement, "My church is doing this; my church is doing that." But the question is: what are you doing? If we are not watching, we become more church-centered, rather than Christ-centered.

Exactly the same thing is true with the Bible. There are people who are Bible-centered, instead of being Christ-centered. If our enemy can get us all wrapped up in our church, in our Bible, in our good works, and keep us from become acquainted with Christ in us, he has brought us to a standstill in our spiritual walk.

Good works is another way the enemy keeps us from a close walk with Jesus. Some people seem to be naturally good people. They are not mean; they are gentle, helpful, and involved in a lot of good things, so they take it for granted that they are okay with God.

The following is a testimony of such a man. This man was very good man; everybody in town would tell you that. He gave of himself freely. He helped the church and worked with the children in town. He would give you a helping hand if you needed it.

When he was quite elderly, he came down with cancer and was placed in a nursing home. Although he did not know the Lord as Savior, he felt God would not reject him because he was such a good man.

Some of the Christian ladies would go to the nursing home to pray for the sick people. Every time they would go, they would pray for him and try to get him to accept Jesus. He was reaching a very critical condition and close to death. Pauline asked me if I would go and talk to him and try to get him to respond to Jesus.

I went with them the next day, and again they talked to him and tried to get him to respond. But he said, "God is not going to reject me; I am a good person!'

The ladies left the room and I stood there talking to the Lord: "Lord, how can I reach this man so that he will understand His need for you?"

The Lord answered: "Tell him all his good works are bunch of dirty rags!"

I said, "Lord, how can I tell him that when he is so sick!"

The Lord replied: "Do you love him? If you do, you will tell him that all his good works are dirty rags."

I went to his bed and knelt down so I was a foot from his face. I looked him right in the eye and said, "All your good works are a bunch of dirty rags!" His eyes got real big and filled with tears and he began to sob.

When he finally got his breath, the first thing he said was, "I need Jesus!" And he received Jesus as his Lord and Savior. The next day he died.

So many things can become stumbling stones, things that seem very good. For this man, his stumbling stone was his years of good works.

For many, the riches of this world and all it has to offer is their stumbling stone. They cannot see beyond the natural. These people cannot see or understand that spiritual things are more valuable than natural things are.

I was out on a small farm in northern Vermont doing an electrical repair job, and I started a conversation with the farmer about his spiritual walk. He became angry right away and told me that he did not want anything to do with the church. And then he went on telling me why: he had been badly injured and offended by a minister.

When he had calmed down, I explained I was not talking about the church, but that I was talking about his relationship with God and with Jesus. He began to listen, and in a little while he accepted Jesus Christ as his personal Savior.

The imperfect church and imperfect minister was this man's stumbling stone. The churches, the priests, and the pastors are not perfect. They are just like you and me—imperfect. Have a lot of grace for these people. Don't be quick to pass judgment, or you will become a stumbling stone.

Jesus may be the greatest stumbling stone of all. Because He called God His Father, many were offended by this, saying, "Who does he think he is, calling God his father?" (see John 5:18)

This next Scripture is also a stumbling stone to many: "Jesus said to him, 'I am the way, and the truth, and the life; no one comes to the Father but through Me.'" (John 14:6)

Many people like to say, "There are other ways to reach God!" But Jesus is the only way, because He is the only one who dealt with the sin issue that separates us from God. Jesus is our sacrificial lamb, and there is no other.

36

Faith Anchor Points

There are certain times, events, and places in our Christian walk that are very important to us. We all have times of distress when we wonder, *God where are you*? The nation of Israel went through this over and over, including the great heroes in the Old Testament. The Lord told them: "Look back, remember the things I have done for you!" I call these faith anchor points.

I remember one of the things God said to me right at the very beginning of the New Life Ministry. He said, "From now on I am your provider!" This word from God anchored deep within me and I have never lost it.

There were times when I forgot it and would look ahead and wonder about the future and start worrying. Then the Holy Spirit would nudge and remind me what God had said to me; instantly faith would rise up and all the fear and worry would depart.

Another one of my faith anchor points are the Scriptures in Joshua 1:6-9. At that time I did not know the Bible at all, so the Lord told me right where to go in the Bible. When I went there, this was the message for me:

> *'Be strong and courageous, for you shall give this people possession of the land which I swore to their fathers to give them. Only be strong and very courageous; be careful to do according to all the law which Moses My servant commanded you; do not turn from it to the right or to the left, so that you may have success wherever you go." (vs. 6-7)*
>
> *"This book of the law shall not depart from your mouth, but you shall meditate on it day and night, so that you may be careful to do according to all that is written in it; for then you will make your way prosperous, and then you will have success. Have I not commanded you? Be strong and courageous! Do not tremble or be dismayed, for the Lord your God is with you wherever you go." (vs. 8-9)*

Many times down through the years when I needed strength and courage to keep going, I have gone back to these Scriptures and every time I would be renewed.

Other anchor points are when God has worked some wonderful miracle or healing in our lives. I remember the time when Pauline had been very sick with a large hard mass as big as a grapefruit in her organs. The doctor told her she needed to go in the hospital right away and have it removed, but because she was filled with poison, they could not do the operation till it was gone. Pauline told the doctor, "Give me what I need to get rid of the poison and then I will go for the operation."

Two days later we had a prayer meeting. We all laid hands on Pauline and prayed for her to be healed. As we prayed, she was slain in the spirit. The Lord spoke to me and said, "She is healed!"

For the next several days, she was worse. Then one morning she went to the bathroom and all the poison came out of her. She bought a new robe for the hospital.

She went back to the doctor again. The doctor was amazed that the big growth was down to the size of a walnut, and said she didn't need to go to the hospital. A couple of weeks later, she went for another check up. This time the mass was totally gone. I think of this miracle often when I pray for others.

I have another faith anchor point that always helps me in the ministry. This one happened at the very beginning of our meetings. When the Lord told me to have a meeting in my home, I said, "Lord, I don't know what to say or do!"

He replied, "I will tell you what to say and what to do!" I remind Him of this before every meeting and He always is there to guide and direct me.

I could go on with other faith anchor points in my life; I have a number of them and I go to them often. They always bless me and encourage me. They still have the same anointing, power, and authority in them as they did forty years ago.

What are your faith anchor points? Do you know what they are? Do you return to them often and let them renew and restore you?

Part Four

From Darkness to Light

37

Great Is The Darkness

> *"If therefore the light that is in you is darkness, how great is the darkness!"— Matthew 6:23*

I have thought about this Scripture many times. Although I still wonder if I understand it, I feel compelled to put down my thoughts. I used to think this Scripture was referring to after we have received some understanding of the Gospel, some revelation from God, and then begin to think that we now have it all. What we previously received becomes a stumbling stone to us, so we cannot receive any more. But I have changed my thinking.

To understand what this Scripture is referring to we must start with Matthew 6:19:

> *"Do not lay up for yourselves treasures upon earth, where moth and rust destroy, and where thieves break in and steal. But lay up for yourselves treasures in heaven, where neither moth nor rust destroys, and where thieves do not break in or steal; for where your treasure is, there your heart will be also."*

We all have our treasures. But what and where they are is the important issue, because our treasures show us where our heart is. According to Jesus, our heart is where our treasure is.

I expect there are some people who do not want to die, because all of their treasures are here on earth and they cannot take them with them. I am sure that these folks are convinced they can see and are filled with light. They would think of you as a fool if you talked about storing up things in heaven for after you die, for they think that death is the end.

One thing I have learned through more than eighty years of life is that whatever I own, owns me and I land up serving it. I am a lot better off just being a good steward of whatever God places me in charge of on this earth and making all my investments in heavenly spiritual places.

My light was darkness for many years. My eye was bad and filled with darkness, and I did not know it. Great was the darkness I was walking and living in. No wonder I stumbled so much; I thought I could see, but my eye was filled with darkness.

> *"The lamp of the body is the eye; if therefore your eye is clear, your whole body will be full of light. But if your eye is bad, your whole body will be full of darkness. If therefore the light that is in you is darkness, how great is the darkness!*
>
> *"No one can serve two masters; for either he will hate the one and love the other, or he will hold to one and despise the other. You cannot serve God and mammon." (Matthew 6:22-24)*

As I was pondering these Scriptures, I realized I had never really given any thought as to what my treasures are or where I am storing them. Our treasures are the things that are valuable to us. They can be money or power and position. They can be a great house or an expensive car and clothes. Or they can be many other things more important than money.

Which brings up another question: are the things I treasure of any value at all? Is my heart set on things that have no value?

What does the light or darkness have to do with what we treasure? If everything we treasure is here on earth, our eye is filled with darkness, and we are not seeing the truth. Even our heart is involved.

What is the desire of your heart? Do you want everything the world has to offer? Money, fame, or position? Do you want to be #1 in everything? To be looked up to? To be the richest person in the world?

The next question is: why do I do those things? Is my heart in them? Or am I just racking up brownie points? What is my heart's desire?

If you desire no more than these things, if these are your heart's desire, then both your eye and your heart are filled with darkness—and how great is that darkness! I expect someone in this position would say, "I see things clearly; I have everything any person would want and am not lacking in anything."

What our heart desires has a big impact on what is important to us. Jesus makes it clear that we cannot serve two masters. So we are left with a question: are my eye and heart filled with light or darkness? Just because we think, "I am filled with light; I believe in God; I go to church and pray every day," does not make it true.

For many people, the church is very dear to their heart. Their church life is very important to them. They love the church. They love the church services. They love the ritual and tradition. But can the church take the place of God? If it does, is our eye and heart filled with darkness?

There are so many religions in the world and I expect they all teach that they have the truth. They say, "We have the light." Millions of people believe it, but the real issue is: "Is my eye filled with light or darkness? What is my heart's desire?"

Knowing that many of our treasures cannot be stored in heaven, my question is: "Which one of my treasures can I store in heaven?"

We have a treasure in earthen vessels; that treasure is a living soul. This is one of the treasures I can store in heavenly places in Christ Jesus. I can also lead other people to Jesus, to be born of the Spirit, and their soul is stored in heavenly places as well.

I believe every time I can become a blessing to someone in need and expect nothing in return, I am storing up another treasure in heaven. Here is a little prayer I have prayed just about every day for years: "Lord, give me the opportunity to be a blessing to someone today."

38

Evil In Me

In Romans 7:21, Paul came out with an interesting statement: *I find then the principle that evil is present in me, the one who wishes to do good.* I have come to the conclusion that I am in the same condition as he is. Evil is always trying to rise up in me, in my speech and in my actions. Yet I have known the Lord for many years and have tried to be faithful and obedient.

I finally asked myself the question: why is evil in me? What is its purpose? Then another question comes to mind: why did God cast Satan down to the earth where the church is?

I believe that Satan was cast down to this earth to fulfill his purpose: to serve God and God's people. In spite of the fact that he waged war in heaven and was defeated, he still must fulfill his purpose. God causes all things to work together for our good, and that includes evil.

When Adam and Eve ate of the fruit from the tree of good and evil, evil became a part of them, and it has been a part of every one of us to this day. If you cannot see that evil is constantly trying to rise up in you and use you, you are indeed blind.

We look around us and see some people who are constantly doing good, while others are doing many evil things. What is the difference between them? The people doing good are refusing to allow the evil in them to rise up and control them. The others are doing nothing to resist the evil that is in them and are letting evil have its way in their lives.

Evil is in us so that we can overcome it and defeat it! If you can defeat the evil in you, then you are truly a victorious person and you have defeated the evil in the world. In effect, you have defeated Satan and all his evil spirits!

There is an interesting Scripture in the Old Testament:

> *... but for Cain and for his offering, He had no regard. So Cain became very angry and his countenance fell.*
> *Then the Lord said to Cain, "Why are you angry? And why has your countenance fallen? If you do well, will not your countenance be lifted up? And if you do not do well, sin is crouching at the door; and its desire is for you, but you must master it." (Genesis 4:5-7)*

It is not the evil out there in the world that defeats you; it is the evil in you that you do not master that defeats you. We can have Christ in us and the baptism of the Holy Spirit and still live in defeat day after day.

Evil has a way of rising up in us so that it does not have the appearance of evil. We think of it as some small sin issue. We then make excuses for our sin, but making excuses for our sin is not a victory. Is murder evil? Is coveting evil? Is gossip evil? Is uncontrolled anger and violence sin or evil? Do these things make our countenance fall?

Who must master it? We do! God through Jesus Christ and the Holy Spirit has given us everything we need to master evil and defeat it.

39

Accuser of the Brethren

The devil, the accuser, has been thrown down to the earth, and he can't leave it. For now the earth is his prison. He is not happy here. He wanted to destroy Jesus, but he was unable to do that. Now he wants to destroy those who have given their lives to Jesus and testify of Him.

> *I heard a loud voice in heaven saying, "Now the salvation, and the power, and the kingdom of our God and the authority of His Christ have come, for the accuser of our brethren has been throne down, who accuses them before our God day and night.*
>
> *And they overcame him because of the blood of the Lamb and because of the word of their testimony, and they did not love their life even to death.*
>
> *For this reason, rejoice, O heavens and you who dwell in them. Woe to the earth, and the sea, because the devil has come down to you, having great wrath, knowing he has only a short time." (Revelation 12:10-12)*

Satan is still the accuser. Who does he accuse and what does he accuse of? The devil accuses us of every sin and mistake we have ever done. He seems to know all of our weaknesses and failures and is constantly bringing them up before us—if we allow it.

Why does he know all these sin areas we have been involved in? Because Satan was right there tempting us into many of them, just like he tempted Adam and Eve. Once he causes us to fall, he turns right around and torments us through accusations. Satan becomes both our tempter and our accuser.

The Bible tells us to guard our thoughts, emotions, and our fleshly desires, because these are the areas the enemy attacks most. If we don't test every thought, Satan is able to put thoughts right into our mind and we think they are our own. If we don't guard our emotions, he fills us with anger, hatred, and all kinds of evil feelings.

Our eyes have a lot to do with worldly desires and fleshly desires. Some things are lovely to look at, but they may not be very good for us.

Satan is not only our accuser; he also very subtly causes us to become accusers. We accuse our neighbors and friends. We accuse our spouse, our children, and our church pastor. And we spend a lot of time accusing ourselves of things we have already been forgiven of.

Jesus had to overcome and defeat Satan, and so do we. How do we do it?

> *And they overcame him because of the blood of the Lamb and because of the word of their testimony, and they did not love their life even to death. (Revelation 12:11)*

Satan is not our only adversary; there are a multitude of fallen angels and evil spirits. They all want to have their way with us. These spirits desire a body, a human body. They don't care if it is healthy or sick. These spirits don't care if it is a child or an old person.

Why do these spirits want a body? Without a body there are very few ways these spirits can manifest themselves in this world. They are just waiting for the opportunity to enter our body. The more control they get in our body, the more they can manifest themselves through our words and actions. Many of them are so subtle, we don't even know we have any—and we may have several.

Many of these spirits are accusing spirits; they spend much time accusing us. When they are not accusing us, they use us to accuse others. As a result, Satan uses us to bring accusation against others, and he doesn't care if it is the truth or a lie.

Satan uses truth to accuse us just as much as he does the lie. These are things we have done in the past that we have repented of, things that have been covered by the blood of the Lamb.

> *And the dragon was enraged with the woman, and went off to make war with the rest of her offspring, who keep the commandments of God and hold to the testimony of Jesus. (Revelation 12:17)*

God has forgotten and forgiven us, but the devil has not. If we do not know our position in Christ and do not use the testimony God has given us, we will continue to be accused all our lives.

40

The Mind and Emotions

Have you ever given much thought to these two special parts of our being—our mind and our emotions? The mind is the center of our thinking process and the heart is the center of our emotional being.

The mind and the emotions are two wonderful blessings from God. All the computers in the world today and the vast knowledge they can store are no comparison to the mind that God has given us. And nothing in this world can compare with our emotions and the range of feelings God has given us! Without them, we would not be able to develop relationships with others. We would not be able to connect emotionally to our loved ones.

We must take care of these wonderful blessings or they will not be in very good condition. As we get older we realize how important our physical body is. If we want to keep it strong and healthy, we start doing things that will keep our body in good condition. For instance, if we have a heart attack, we are suddenly aware of how important the heart is, and hopefully we begin to take better care of it.

After several years of ministry, one of the things I have noticed is that some people are controlled by their emotions. Others are controlled by their mind. Still others seem to be pretty much controlled by their sense of well-being. But none of these should be controlling us—we should be controlling our mind and our emotions.

If our mind and emotions are not to control us, then how will we have any control? We are to be spirit-controlled, because our spirit is the highest part of our being.

A sad thing happened when Adam and Eve were disobedient. God had to remove them from the garden; this had a terrible effect on the mind and heart of man. Ever since, people have had troubled minds and hearts.

Why would God have to do such a thing? If God had allowed Adam and Eve had to remain in the garden and eat from that tree of life, they would have had eternal life in a body that was dying from having eaten the poisoned fruit!

Since the Garden, these wonderful gifts from God—the mind and the emotions—can be used for good or for evil. The choice is ours. Some people use their mind to think of ways to rob people and take advantage of them. There are others who use their mind to think up ways to bless a lot of people.

Emotions are the same way; we can see this day after day on the TV or news. A few people can stir up thousands of people in an emotional frenzy, and others can touch people with compassion, love, and forgiveness. This shows us that we can be very easily controlled and manipulated by others, if we are not guarding our mind and emotions.

The mind and emotions are like a piano—they can be played. So if you don't keep the piano closed, someone is going to come along and play a melody on it. Lock it and make sure you are the only one who plays on your piano.

Truly this is an amazing thing! What an awesome power God has put into our keeping when He gave us a mind and emotions. He also tells us that we are responsible for our words and actions.

> *"The good man out of the good treasure of his heart brings forth what is good; and the evil man out of the evil treasure brings forth what is evil; for his mouth speaks from that which fills his heart." (Luke 6: 45)*

Other people can really affect our mind and emotions, but the problem does not end there. The spiritual beings in this world can also affect them. If we do not guard our heart and mind, lying deceiving thoughts and emotions will somehow get in and torment us day and night.

For though we walk in the flesh, we do not war according to the flesh, for the weapons of our warfare are not of the flesh, but divinely powerful for the destruction of fortresses.
We are destroying speculations and every lofty thing raised up against the knowledge of God, and we are taking every thought captive to the obedience of Christ. (2 Corinthians 10:3-5)

There are some who have been told and taught that a Christian cannot be troubled by an evil spirit. This is just what the enemy wants us to think. If this is the truth, why do we have so many troubled Christian people?

Who is the enemy that Satan is waging war with? The church! How does he wage this war? With evil spirits, fallen angels, principalities, powers of darkness and others.

What is he waging war against? Our heart and mind! He also attacks our body with spiritual infirmities and diseases. We have seen many Christians healed by taking authority over the spirit of sickness and diseases and commanding it to go in the name of Jesus Christ.

The mind is remarkable. It is our communication center; it handles the communications between you and me, and the communications between God and us. It also handles the communications between evil spirits and us.

Sometimes we hear of someone losing their mind. What a terrible thing to happen, losing something so valuable. Most of us take good care of the things that are valuable to us, like our money and riches, but our mind is more valuable. We need to realize how valuable it is and do everything in our power to protect it.

Our emotions can be so strong and powerful and yet so fragile. They can be injured so easily, but do you realize the blessings that emotions give us? What kind of relationships can we have without our emotions? We could not develop relationships without them.

Think of the range of emotions you go through each day and how they affect you. Note that your emotions can change moment by moment, from sadness to happiness, guilt to forgiveness, and anger to joy. Your emotions can change just from what is going on around you, like going to church, enjoying the comfort of home, driving on the highway, your work environment, prayer, or going to a movie. Many things can touch our emotions.

Emotional well-being is important to your bodily health and to your mind. Your emotions can be healthy or sick. You can give away love, joy, and peace, or you can also give away anger, depression, and other awful things.

Because we can give these things away, we can also receive them. Have you ever walked into someone's house and felt the anger that was there? The oppression or heaviness that was there? It was your emotional being that gave you the ability to feel those things.

Not only can we feel our own emotions, but we can feel the emotions of others around us. It is very important that we have discernment to tell the difference between our own emotions and the emotions coming from other sources.

Have you experienced God's love, peace and joy? Have you experienced love and joy coming from another person? Our emotions give us the ability to feel emotions coming from other places, from an individual or a group of people.

We must guard our heart and mind, but we must be discerning and allow some of the emotions around us to touch us, like love, peace, and joy. But there are other emotions that you do not want to touch you—negative emotions like anger, hatred, bitterness, resentment and others.

We must guard our emotions, because many of them could be right in our own home, from people close to us. Some people have very strong negative emotions, and if you do not have a strong defense system, you need to stay away from them or they overpower you.

In my first encounter with God, I experienced peace from God. It touched me very deeply. That peace brought healing to my body, soul and spirit, and He has never taken it away. Later on in my Christian journey, the Lord told me I could give that peace to other people.

Every now and then the Holy Spirit would direct me to give that peace away to someone who was in need of it. I would lay my hand on them and say, "The peace of the Lord be with you," and they would be filled with peace on the spot. I have now learned that I have some wonderful things to give away: love, peace and joy, and all the fruit of the Holy Spirit.

Our mind and emotions are two very wonderful and powerful things. If we allow the Holy Spirit to teach us how to use them fully, we can bring a lot of healing to those around us.

41

Senses and Awareness

In the animal kingdom, senses and awareness are vital issues. If they do not learn to use them at an early age, they do not live long. Senses and awareness are important to us as well. If we do not learn to use them at an early age, we will go through all kinds of problems and difficulties we could have avoided.

I can see now that if I would have paid attention to what my senses and awareness were telling me, I would have stayed away from some people and some places. But I was not sensible and I was totally unaware. I know we cannot be aware of everything going on in the world, yet there are many things we should be aware of that affect us and our church and family.

We do not have to know everything, but our senses and awareness need to be working. In the armed services when there is combat, they know that the greatest number will be killed the first few days. If a man can survive those first days, there is a good chance he will survive a long time. What is at work here? He is using his senses and awareness, and they keep him alive.

As Christian people, we have natural senses and spiritual senses. We must learn to use both. We find in the Scriptures that God at times has hardened men's hearts. I believe what has happened is that He has dulled their senses and awareness. If we resist God when He is trying to show us truth, our conscience is seared and we are unable to receive truth.

> *You foolish Galatians, who has bewitched you, before whose eyes Jesus Christ was publicly portrayed as crucified? (Galatians 3:1)*

Why were these people bewitched? They were not aware of the difference between spirituality and man's religion. These people were not using their spiritual senses. They were totally unaware they were being misled; they did not recognize that a person was deceiving and misleading them. I expect the people who were doing the bewitching did not even know they were doing it—the blind leading the blind. This is still happening in some of our churches today.

Concerning him we have much to say, and it is hard to explain, since you have become dull of hearing. (Hebrews 5:11)

Who is it that they could not hear? Jesus the high priest!

At one time these people could hear and understand spiritual things. Now they had lost that ability. Their natural hearing had not failed, but it was their spiritual hearing or senses that had become dull.

For many people going to church is like a dream experience. Why is it like a dream? Many people know they dreamed, but they cannot recall the dream. The church experience is similar in that not everyone can recall the message that was given.

Dreams come from the unconscious mind, not the natural mind. We do not retain the dream unless we place it in the natural mind's memory. The reason for this is that the dream comes from a different source and the natural memory does not record it.

When we wake up, if we would instantly spend some time thinking about the dream with our natural mind, the memory will then be retained. The same thing would happen if people, when leaving the church, would think about the message they heard and even talk about it. They would, in turn, retain the message.

It is rather interesting that gossipers have sharp ears and retain everything.

We are more interested in expressing our thoughts than we are in listening to what someone else has to say. It takes training to still our mind and really listen to what others have to say. Many of us have become experts at blocking out things we don't want to hear. This has probably contributed to our dullness of hearing.

A new mother is a wonderful example of how sensitive a person can become when there is a baby to watch over; all their senses and awareness become acute at this time in their life.

When we become Christians, our spiritual senses can function. We can begin to see and hear spiritual things. We must exercise these senses so that we can hear and be led by the Holy Spirit.

Good students really pay attention to the teacher, and they have very good study habits. They are not necessarily any smarter than a poor student, but they are using all their senses and awareness. So it is in the church; we have good students and poor students.

> *But solid food is for the mature, who because of practice have their senses trained to discern good and evil. (Hebrews 5:14)*

God has given us all the abilities we need to follow Him and to serve Him. Do we also have the abilities to sense and be aware of evil spirits when they are in our homes and troubling us or our children?

Yes! We should know as soon as an evil spirit enters our home or troubles our family, and we should be quick to do something about it.

How do we know when an evil spirit is troubling our family?

We feel uncomfortable. Things are not going right around the house. People are bickering and out of sorts. There is heaviness in our spirit. It will seem as if the peace left and joy has gone from our home. These are all good signs that there is a spirit messing up our house.

Most Christians are unable to do anything about this sad condition. They lack the knowledge God has given us and the church authorities over these spirits. They don't know how to use this spiritual authority.

The kingdom of God has come with all kinds of blessings, but we do not take advantage of most of them, because of our lack of knowledge.

42

Stinking Thinking

Finally, brethren, whatever is true, whatever is honorable, whatever is right, whatever is pure, whatever is lovely, whatever is of good repute, if there is any excellence and if anything worthy of praise, let your mind dwell on these things.—Philippians 4:8

I had a very strange dream one night. I was standing before a small group of people. There were also several small animals with the group. There was a large man who seemed to be the center figure of the group. Something seemed to be very strange about his head.

I could see an opening right across his forehead. It looked like some small animals were in the opening in his head. Then he put his hands up to his head and two small animals came out into his hands. A few moments later, they went right back into his head. These little animals looked like skunks. At this point I woke up.

The next day I shared this dream with Pauline and two other friends, and right away they said, "stinking thinking!" As I gave more thought to this dream, I realized it was speaking of the natural mind. We have a natural mind as well as a spiritual mind, like the mind of Christ.

Two days later, I had another dream. In this dream the earth was coming to an end. They were loading people on space ships and sending them off to some other planets, but there were not enough space ships to take everyone.

Then someone came up with the idea of using airplanes for space ships in order to try and save the ones left behind. Pauline and I were part of the group who were left behind, so we were loaded onto an airplane and sent off into space, hoping we would survive.

The scene changed. We were now on a ship on the ocean. The ship came to an island and stopped there for some reason. Pauline and I got off the ship to check out the island. We walked a long way to the other end of the island, and then came back. Just as we reached a place where we could see the ship, what looked like a huge whirlwind grabbed the ship and rolled it over and over and the ship sank.

We realized everything we owned was on that ship and we had nothing but the clothes on our backs. I thought, "I have my credit cards," but then I remembered that the earth was gone and so were all the banks, so the credit cards were worthless. We were left with nothing.

I turned around and started walking back down the island and thought, *what will we do now*? I turned to Pauline and said, "I know what we will do: we will preach Jesus Christ and Him crucified!" The dream ended.

As soon as I woke up, I started thinking about the dream. I knew that both dreams were giving the same message, and then a Scripture came to mind:

> *For I determined to know nothing among you except Jesus Christ and Him crucified. (1 Corinthians 2:2).*

Why was "Jesus Christ and Him crucified" so important that Paul left everything behind to preach that message?

I remember a little incident that took place a couple of years ago. We were in a restaurant having lunch. A man was waiting on us, and I asked him if he knew Jesus. He said, "Yes, he is standing right over there in the lounge."

That was not the answer I expected, but then I realized I was in a Mexican restaurant and many Mexican people are named Jesus. I also remembered being in Egypt, and the people there made a point of telling us that Jesus had spent some time there. They believed in Jesus as a prophet but not as the Christ who was crucified. This made me think of a reading in 2 Corinthians 11:4:

For if one comes and preaches another Jesus whom we have not preached, or you receive a different spirit which you have not received, or a different gospel which you have not accepted, you bear this beautifully.

Then I realized what was so important about Jesus Christ and Him crucified: it was the sin issue. He was the only one who has died for our sins!

What does "stinking thinking" have to do with Jesus and Him crucified? Many Christian people believe they are going to continue to sin and fail over and over again. They don't understand that Jesus not only died for their sin, but He also set us free from the bondage of sin, so we do not have to continue sinning any longer.

What shall we say then? Are we to continue in sin that grace might increase? May it never be! How shall we who died to sin still live in it? (Romans 6:1-2)

We have no excuse to continue in sin anymore, because Jesus Christ and the cross freed us from the bondage of sin. We have the helper, guide, and teacher, the Holy Spirit, here to lead us out of the darkness into the light. We can now walk in holiness and godliness. St. Peter did such a wonderful job of laying out the path for us in the Scriptures:

Simon Peter, a bond-servant and apostle of Jesus Christ, to those who have received a faith of the same kind as ours, by the righteousness of our God and Savior, Jesus Christ: Grace and peace be multiplied to you in the knowledge of God and of Jesus our Lord; seeing that His divine power has granted to us everything pertaining to life and godliness, through the true knowledge of Him who called us by His own glory and excellence.

For by these He has granted to us His precious and magnificent promises, in order that by them you might become partakers of the divine nature, having escaped the corruption that is in the world by lust.

Now for this very reason also, applying all diligence, in your faith supply moral excellence, and in your moral excellence, knowledge; and in your knowledge, self-control, and in your self-control, perseverance,

> *and in your perseverance, godliness; and in your godliness, brotherly kindness, and in your brotherly kindness, love.*
>
> *For if these qualities are yours and are increasing, they render you neither useless nor unfruitful in the true knowledge of our Lord Jesus Christ. For he who lacks these qualities, is blind or short-sighted, having forgotten his purification from his former sins.* (2 Peter 1:1-9)

As long as I keep professing that I am a sinner, I will continue to sin. When I begin to believe that Jesus has totally dealt with all my sin, set me totally free from sin bondage, and start believing that I do not have to live in sin anymore, I become a free man. I then enter into a new place of peace and rest, with no condemnation.

The stinking thinking is left behind.

43

Images

Then God said, "Let Us make man in Our image, according to Our likeness: and let them rule over the fish of the sea and over the birds of the sky and over the cattle and over all the earth, and every creeping thing that creeps on the earth."—Genesis 1:26

Man has also become an image-maker. We like to make images of God. We like to make images of each other. We carve them in stone, paint pictures, or use cameras and other high tech equipment. Making images is a part of our life. But every image is not a good image. Some images need to be torn down and destroyed.

One of the difficulties with images is that we can come to worship them. This has happened many times down through the ages. When an image becomes too important to us, it becomes holy ground. If anyone dares touch it or defile it, we protect it in any way we can.

We have holy images all over the earth; some of them are buildings, some are cows or other animals, and some are statues. Now it seems that man is trying to be God and make God in our image. I don't think that is very wise.

What images do we need to destroy?

Professing to be wise, they became fools, and exchanged the glory of the incorruptible God for an image in the form of corruptible man and of birds and four-footed animals and crawling creatures.

Therefore God gave them over in the lust of their hearts to impurity, that their bodies might be dishonored among them.

For they exchanged the truth of God for a lie, and worshipped and served the creature rather than the Creator, who is blessed forever. Amen. (Romans 1:22-25)

It is not just the physical images around us that create a problem for us and bring pressure to bear on our lives. The images we build up in our minds are just as powerful, if not more so. These inner images are very destructive to our lives.

We can project these images on to others. As parents, we can build up images of our children and project them on to our children. If they cannot live up to the images, they are injured and we are disappointed. Many times we have ministered to married couples whose marriage was failing because they were not able to live up to the images they had for each other. If we could make them see that this was their problem, they could break the image and go on with their marriage.

It is important we recognize images for what they are and not allow them to have any power over us. Images only have the power that we give them. For years I was trying to be the image of someone else and running away from what I really was. What a relief when I finally saw that and stopped running after other images.

Man seems to be naturally religious. When we do not have a relationship with a spiritual God who is invisible to our eyes, then we want to make one. We look to the sun, the moon and the stars, or to another person who seems to be much greater than ourselves. Even worse, our inflated ego can begin to project, "I am God," and we worship our own image.

44

Imaginations

When God made us in His image, He gave us a lot of responsibility over the world and all that was in it. However, I think that our greatest responsibility is not over the world but over our self as an individual. How well do I function with myself and with the people around me?

The imagination is active in many people, if not all people. *The American Heritage Dictionary* describes "imagination" in this way: "The power of the mind to form a mental image or concept of something that is not real or present." And old meaning of the imagination is a plotting or a devising of evil. Another meaning much used in the Bible is stubbornness. There are many negative admonitions in the Bible concerning the imagination.

The imagination is a powerful tool that can be used for good or for evil. We must use it carefully and keep it under control. It seems like the least little thing can cause the imagination to become active.

> *For those who are according to the flesh set their minds on the things of the flesh, but those who are according to the Spirit, the things of the Spirit. For the mind set on the flesh is death, but the mind set on the Spirit is life and peace. (Romans 8:5-6)*

This Scripture makes clear the difference between the flesh and the Spirit. God gives us total freedom as to which level we want to function at. If we set our mind on the things above, our imaginations are going to be filled with life. If we set our mind on the things of the flesh, our imaginations are going to be fleshly.

From the time I was a little kid, I have been a daydreamer. When I became a teenager, my imaginations were not so very nice. When I experienced Christ in my life, I started thinking spiritually and my imaginations changed. At this point, God used my imagination to teach me and to bring me many wonderful healings.

One of the dangers of imagination is that, if we dwell on our imaginations too long, they take on a life of their own and become more real to us than the real world. These imaginations are very difficult, hard to get freed from. Our imaginations are an outworking of our thought life. Control your thought life and you have control of your imaginations.

45

Yes or No

"But let your statement be, 'Yes, yes' or 'No, no'; and anything beyond this is of evil."—Matthew 5:37

Have you ever made excuses? I expect most of you have made quite a few excuses. Why do we feel that we have to make excuses?

Did you notice we make excuses when we have to say no to someone or to something? We don't make excuses when we say yes! Why do we have to make excuses when we say no? As a rule, it is because the other person wants to know why we said no. They say, "Why can't you do this? You have the time, the expertise. You know how we need you." And on and on they go.

Jesus said, let your yes be yes, and your no be no. We can't settle for that. God can, but we can't. We have to make up excuses. Then we feel uncomfortable with our excuses, because most of the time they are not the truth.

From the time we are little children, we do not want to accept no for an answer. Our children don't want to accept no either. Every time we use the word *no,* we have to go on the defensive, because we know that we are going to come under attack.

When we have a good reason for saying no and try to explain it, most people don't want to hear what we have to say. They still think we are making a lame excuse. It's one of those situations where you can't win.

There are others who are unable to say no, so they become involved in all kind of programs and works that they really don't have time for and should not be involved in. And then there are those people who say yes to everything, but they have no intention of doing anything or following through on anything.

We find that we can be yes-people or no-people, but one is just as big a problem as the other. This has something to do with our integrity and truthfulness.

Hopefully we come to a place where we are sick of having to make excuses or lying. We can say no and refuse to make any excuses. We can say yes, knowing we will try our best to fulfill our commitments.

Remember, Jesus taught: "Let your yes be yes or your no be no."

46

Memories

What a wonderful gift God gave to us when He created us with memory. Pauline and I have traveled to a lot of interesting places. We have taken many great pictures. I often sit at the computer and scroll through these pictures. Each picture I look at opens up a memory; some of them are very pleasant.

Every one of us has thousands of memories, maybe millions, I suppose. It reminds me of the storage places we see along the highway where people store stuff away, sometimes for many years. I can see millions of little storage places inside of me, each one of them with a memory inside of it waiting to be opened some day.

Within each one of these memories other things are stored, like joy, peace, love, and also suffering, grief, sorrow, pain, and even fear and terror. There are certain things that unlock these memories, like when I look at the pictures of our travels and experience pleasure and joy.

Some of these memories we never want to open because they are filled with pain and fear. There are things that happen in our daily lives that suddenly open some of these memories and we experience the pain and terror all over again. These kinds of memories need to be healed because the pain, anguish, and fear that remain locked inside of them affect our health and well-being, and rob us of our peace and joy.

A way of dealing with these bad memories is to open them up and ask Jesus Christ to enter the memory with you and remove the pain, fear, and whatever other energy is still in there. I use the word energy because that is what these bad memories contain. Once the energy is removed, the memory still remains but it cannot trouble you anymore.

Sometimes we can deal with these bad memories through prayer and inviting Jesus to enter them with us. Often we need the help of someone else who is knowledgeable in this type of ministry. Working with Jesus Christ and the Holy Spirit we can be free of these bad memories that have haunted and troubled us for years.

Drugs and medicine cannot heal these memories. Jesus Christ and the Holy Spirit can, if we recognize we need help in this area. As we continue on in our spiritual journey, we need to get cleansing and healing in our memories.

47

Self-Control

One particular problem that most of us are acquainted with is our tongue.

For we all stumble in many ways. If anyone does not stumble in what He says, he is a perfect man, able to bridle the whole body as well. (James 3:2)

So also the tongue is a small part of the body, and yet it boasts of great things. Behold, how great a forest is set aflame by such a small fire! And the tongue is a fire, the very world of iniquity; the tongue is set among our members as that which defiles the entire body, and sets on fire the course of our life, and is set on fire by hell. (James 3:5-6)

But no one can tame the tongue; it is a restless evil and full of deadly poison. (James 3:8)

The tongue is a part of our flesh and it is evil—we cannot tame it! The only thing we can do is bridle it to control it. The minute we take the bridle off, it is out of control.

A good example of this is on Sunday morning. It is so easy to get upset with someone before going to church. We get angry and sound off, then we are off to church. We arrive and now we are in control. We smile and speak nicely to everyone. And we control our thoughts and emotions and our speech.

Then church lets out and we want to leave quickly, but the other cars are in our way and traffic is slow. It is easy at this point to lose control, think differently, and speak differently. This can happen any day of the week, at home or out in public.

One of the things that causes us to lose control is stress. Another is anger. If we allow bitterness and resentment to have its way, it will move right into our emotions and make its home there. It will cause some bad things to come out of our mouth, and these things will reach out and injure people around us.

There are some who say that this kind of thing doesn't happen to real Christians, but it does. It happens to too many Christians every day. It can happen to any one of us—at any time. We have an enemy who is waiting for the opportunity to have its way with our tongue. Bridle it and control it!

When we allow our mind and emotions to control us, we do and say things that later we regret: we think that was a stupid thing to do or say. We find that we need some way to control these thoughts and emotions.

We also know some of our thoughts and emotions are very strong and difficult to control. As wonderful as these abilities are, some people are destroyed by them, and some people are using them to destroy others.

The Bible teaches us that there is a way to control these things. It is called self-control; another way of saying it is control of self. We need some way of controlling our self. But in the following Scriptures, Peter is telling us that self-control alone is still not enough: we must have faith, moral excellence, knowledge, perseverance, godliness, brotherly kindness and love.

> *... seeing that His divine power has granted to us everything pertaining to life and godliness, through the true knowledge of Him who called us by His own glory and excellence.*
>
> *For by these He has granted to us His precious and magnificent promises, in order that by them you might become partakers of the divine nature, having escaped the corruption that is in the world by lust.*
>
> *Now for this very reason also, applying all diligence, in your faith supply moral excellence, and in your moral excellence, knowledge; and in your knowledge, self-control, and in your self-control, perseverance, and in your perseverance, godliness; and in your godliness, brotherly kindness, and in your brotherly kindness, love. (2 Peter 1:3-7)*

There is a victory for us. Jesus has made the way clear. Our victory is to become spiritually mature men and women led by the Spirit, controlling our fleshly desires, our mind, and our emotions: it is called self-control.

48

Righteousness

For the kingdom of God is not eating and drinking, but righteousness and peace and joy in the Holy Spirit—Romans 14:17

The Holy Spirit brought me to this Scripture many years ago. I spent some time pondering what the Holy Spirit wanted me to see in this. The part that really stood out for me was the word *righteousness*.

I knew that Jesus Christ is our righteousness, but He wanted me to see something more. I finally saw that He wanted me to be righteous. If I wanted the peace and joy, I had to be righteous. Maybe a better way of putting it is that I had to feel right about myself.

I expect that every one of you at some time have felt wrong about yourself or about others; you said the wrong thing or did the wrong thing. Did you like that feeling afterwards? I think not!

At other times you felt right; you said the right thing or did the right thing. Did you like that? I am sure you did. This is the kind of righteousness I am speaking of; this is what the Holy Spirit wanted me to see.

As I began to think about this, I realized it was important for me to be righteous if I wanted to be healthy in my mind, heart, and spirit. How blessed is the righteous person! But note that this is not the same as self-righteous. When we are self-righteous, we are proud. When we are righteous, we are humble.

The wonderful thing about righteousness is the peace and joy that go with it. The individuals who have found this kind of righteousness become a blessing to all those around them. They are speaking and acting properly with God. They are speaking and acting right with the people around them, at home and at work.

How blessed are these people, for they will have peace and joy, and they will be a blessing to those around them.

The Lord is far from the wicked, but He hears the prayer of the righteous. (Proverbs 15:29)

49

Interpreting Life

Who has the true interpretation? This is a question that has troubled many people, church hierarchies, and religious organizations down through the years. Wars have been fought; nations have been divided; people have been imprisoned and put to death; families have been divided and have nothing to do with one another. The Christian church has been divided over and over, hundreds of times, because of this question, and it is still divided today.

I experienced the Lord in an interesting way. My life was falling apart and I went into a church and got down on my face and asked God to help me. Nobody instructed me or told me the words to pray. I was alone in the church. This could have happened anywhere; I did not have to be in a church.

I knew nothing. I did not know the Bible. I knew very little about the church I went to. I can't say that I really understood what happened to me that day. All I knew was it changed me, and that I had received healing and was set free. From that day I went on with my life.

For seven years I didn't tell a soul what had happened to me in that church that day. I didn't read the Bible or even pray any more than I did before. But something was happening to me—I was changing.

One of the major changes was the relationship between Pauline and me. It was as if the animosity was gone between us. We were functioning now as a family, not as two people who were each trying to be the winner.

Another change was in my relationship to church. I was enjoying the church more and was beginning to understand what the service was all about. The changes were slow but continued for the next seven years.

Notice that no one was trying to teach us how to be good Christians. We were not reading the Bible. We went to church some of the time, but not always—yet we were changing. Now I know why! Jesus and the Holy Spirit were at work in us.

I am sure that some of you must be thinking, what does this have to do with interpretation? First I want to explain what "interpret" and "interpretation" mean according to the dictionary. To interpret means to tell or explain the meaning in understandable terms or to act as an interpreter between speakers of different languages.

Interpretation refers to an explanation or a proper understanding of things. For example, ten people are looking at a painting, and then each one shares what the painting is saying to them. I expect everyone would interpret the picture a little differently; none of them would see it the way the artist sees it. Interpretation can also refer to a teaching technique that stresses appreciation and understanding.

Now I understand that in those first seven years, Jesus and the Holy Spirit were interpreting a whole new way of living to Pauline and me. They were teaching; we were learning.

But the process took place not by the world's teachers or even religious teachers, but by the Holy Spirit Himself. He was giving us a new understanding of life. This is what Christianity should be to all of us: a whole new way of life!

After those first seven years, things changed once again. I was prayed over to be baptized in the Holy Spirit. Right away some of you might say, "You already had the Holy Spirit!"

You are right. I already had the Holy Spirit, but what we must recognize is that we are anointed by the Holy Spirit more than once in our lifetime—for different purposes. This time the Holy Spirit baptized me with a new power and authority for ministry.

Before this, I did not have any desire to read the Bible, but from that time on I did. I had a great hunger to read the Bible, and I would read it till late at night. I had a Bible that had the commentaries at the bottom of each page. I intended to use them to help me understand the Scriptures, but that was not God's plan. When I started to read those commentaries, the Holy Spirit said, "No! You are not to read any commentaries."

I asked Him why not. He replied, "I don't want you knowing other people's interpretation; I want to give you my interpretation. You just read and I will give you understanding." This is what I did for several years.

One day, as I was reading the New Testament, I came to these verses in John 14:26:

> *"But the Helper, the Holy Spirit, whom the Father will send in My name, He will teach you all things, and bring to your remembrance all that I said to you."*

We have many teachers in the body of Christ. But since the churches don't agree on many things, this can leave us in a state of confusion. One person sees a Scripture one way, but another person sees it in a different way. The question is: who is right and who is wrong?

Perhaps they may be both right. We need to recognize that each one may be in a different circumstance, and the Holy Spirit is giving them a different understanding to fit their circumstances. The Scriptures are not dead words—they are filled with life and meaning. It is the Holy Spirit who is the interpreter of the *living* word; no man can do it like the Holy Spirit can.

We all need to learn to interpret well. When I give a teaching or a message, I try to make it as clear and simple as I possibly can. I have been amazed when I talk to people after I give a talk and ask them what they heard or thought I was saying. They would tell me something totally different than what I thought I was saying. They interpreted the message different from what I intended. If you asked ten people or a hundred people, I expect they would all interpret the message a little differently.

Interpretation is going on in our life every day. Life is saying something to us all the time, and we are interpreting it for the good or for the bad. How each one of us interprets life every moment is very important, because our interpretation can be our friend or our enemy.

How we interpret God is important. Do we think He is for us or against us? Is my spouse for me or against me? Is this person my friend or my enemy? The way we see things and understand things, the way we interpret things, is very important.

May God help all of us to interpret and understand life so that we can live it to its fullest.

Part Five

The Spiritual Realm

50

Born Again, Convert, Conversion

These are three very important words in our Christian walk: born again, convert, conversion. What do they mean to you? I believe it is important that each one of us know what these words mean to us, because our spiritual eternal life is at stake.

These words mean something totally different to me now than they did when I was thirty-two years old. Back then, if someone spoke of being born again, I figured they were crazy. If they talked to me about conversion, I thought they wanted me to join another church. If they spoke about being a convert, I figured they must have changed churches.

I didn't have the foggiest idea that they were talking about becoming a spiritual person and having a personal experience with Jesus Christ. I could relate to Nicodemus in the Gospel of John. These Scriptures are a profound truth. If we can understand them, we are well on our way into the kingdom of God.

> *Now there was a man of the Pharisees, named Nicodemus, a ruler of the Jews; this man came to Him by night, and said to Him, "Rabbi, we know that You have come from God as a teacher; for no one can do these signs that You do unless God is with him."*
>
> *Jesus answered and said to him, "Truly, truly, I say to you, unless one is born again, he cannot see the kingdom of God."*
>
> *Nicodemus said to Him, "How can a man be born when he is old? He cannot enter a second time into his mother's womb and be born, can he?"*
>
> *Jesus answered, "Truly, truly, I say to you, unless one is born of water and the Spirit, he cannot enter into the kingdom of God. That which is born of the flesh is flesh, and that which is born of the Spirit is spirit." (John 3:1-6)*

I now realize that until we are born again of the Spirit, we cannot understand what a born again experience is. If you ask a person, "Have you ever had an experience with God?" they know how to answer you yes or no. Yet many people have had a born again experience with God, but because of a lack of knowledge of what being born again is, they still have no understanding of it.

I remember my brother sharing with me what happened to him and how he came to experience the Holy Spirit. A salesman stopped by his house one day and started talking to him and asked him if he had experienced God. My brother said, "What do you mean, experience God?"

The man said, "You were married?"

My brother said, "Yes."

The salesman replied, "That is an experience. This is what you should have with God."

As a result, my brother and several other people began searching for an experience with God. Some time later he had an experience with God in a small church in Canada when the pastor gave an alter call. My brother went forward and he had a life-changing experience with God. But before this happened, my brother was in the same position as many other church people are in: he had experienced church, but he had never experienced God.

He, like many others, had tried several other churches and religions, trying to find something that was missing. What was missing was the spiritual relationship with God, but this only comes through the born-again experience with Jesus Christ.

At times, the Holy Spirit will lead us to be involved in other churches, and sometimes He will keep us away from churches and organized religion. Why would He do this? Maybe so we would spend some time with Him instead of the church. There are times we become more reliant on the church and religion than we are on Him. I realize now that for some people the organized religions take the place of a relationship with God.

We can convert from being a Catholic to being a Baptist, or from a Baptist to a Mormon, and learn a whole new way of worship and different rituals, but still not be any closer to God. We find that church and ritual are also an experience, but they are not a born-again experience.

A convert speaks more of a change of religion than he or she does of a born-again experience. They learn a new way of doing things. The service may be different and exciting—a new set of theology, new rituals and traditions, new music, new forms of worship, new people—yet all of this can be another religious experience and not spiritual at all. So we can have religious experiences as well as spiritual experiences, but without discernment, it is hard to know the difference.

Another experience we can have is with another spirit who is not the Holy Spirit. This other spirit tries to copy the Holy Spirit and makes us think we have had a valid conversion experience.

Keeping in mind all these things, how can I know I am born-again and experienced a real conversion? The Bible says you will know them by their fruit. What fruit? The fruit of the Holy Spirit: faith, love, joy and peace.

When a true conversion happens, it is not a change of church, dogma or ritual, but you are given a new heart. You are not the same anymore—you have increased. Your spirit has come alive in a new wonderful way. You do not have to try to change; you will change!

After a true conversion, some changes take place. You desire to know more about God and to have an intimate relationship with Him. You have a desire to read the Scriptures, to talk with God, and to pray more. You have a greater awareness of God's presence with you and in you.

Another thing that happens is we begin to see and understand things differently. The Scriptures have new meaning for us, and we see and understand them more clearly. Sin becomes more sinful. We see the self-righteousness and pride that is in us, and we don't like it; we begin to experience humility.

These things don't happen overnight, but you see enough of the changes so you realize something wonderful has happened to you. You have times when God's love, peace, and joy overwhelm you; and other times, when you wonder where He is, but He never leaves you. These are some of the things that take place when we have a true conversion, a born-again experience.

51

The Kingdom of God – A Place of Peace

The kingdom of God is now available to us through Jesus Christ. There is no other way of reaching or entering the kingdom of God, apart from Jesus and the cross. Multitudes choose to believe there are other ways to enter, but there isn't.

The reason we cannot enter apart from Jesus Christ is sin; the kingdom of God is pure and undefiled. The key to the kingdom is Jesus Christ and His death on the cross. If you cannot accept that, you will never enter in.

You can do all kinds of good works and go to church every day. You can become a priest, a minister, or a Catholic Sister and pray all day, but that will not get you in. Your sin must be atoned for, and you cannot pay the price for the least sin you ever did.

The kingdom of God is a spiritual kingdom. It is not of this world, but it is in this world. It is within us and all around us, but most of us are unaware of it. This kingdom is in us, but sadly most of us are not in it. This wonderful place called the kingdom of God is a place of peace, joy, righteousness and the Holy Spirit.

> *... for the kingdom of God is not eating and drinking, but righteousness and peace and joy in the Holy Spirit. (Romans 14:17)*

Some people find and enter into the kingdom of God while they are still living. Within these people, you can see the joy and the peace they have.

There is a Scripture that reads, "*Be still and know that I am God.*" If we can become still, it is in the stillness we begin to become aware of the kingdom of God. It is in the stillness we become aware of God's angels who are around us all of the time. It is in the stillness we begin to recognize God's thoughts right in our mind and His love right in our heart.

Because we find this wonderful place of peace, it doesn't mean that we stop living in this world; the opposite might be true. Even though we become more active than we ever were before, we can keep our peace in the midst of the world and whatever it throws at us.

We now have eternal life with our Savior and nothing can take it away from us. Death is only a shadow, and we have no fear of it any longer. There is no death for us in the kingdom of God.

52

Law and Faith

When the Lord called me into this work and ministry, the following Scriptures were given to me by the Holy Spirit. Since I did not know the Bible, the Holy Spirit directed me to the following book and verses in Joshua 1:5-9:

> *No man will be able to stand before you all the days of your life. Just as I have been with Moses, I will be with you; I will not fail you or forsake you.*
>
> *Be strong and courageous, for you shall give this people possession of the land which I swore to their fathers to give them. Only be strong and very courageous; be careful to do according to all the law which Moses My servant commanded you; do not turn from it to the right or to the left, so that you may have success wherever you go.*
>
> *This book of the law shall not depart from your mouth, but you shall meditate on it day and night, so that you may be careful to do according to all that is written in it; for then you will make your way prosperous, and then you will have success.*
>
> *Have I not commanded you? Be strong and courageous! Do not tremble or be dismayed, for the Lord your God is with you wherever you go. (vs. 8-9)*

On the same day, He directed me to another Scripture in Acts 26:16-18:

> *"But arise and stand on your feet; for this purpose I have appeared to you, to appoint you a minister and a witness not only to the things which you have seen, but also to the things in which I will appear to you;*
>
> *"Delivering you from the Jewish people and from the Gentiles, to whom I am sending you, to open their eyes so that they may turn from darkness to light and from the dominion of Satan to God, in order that they may receive forgiveness of sins and an inheritance among those who have been sanctified by faith in Me."*

In both of these Scriptures, God was calling Joshua and Paul into His service. When I read these Scriptures, God was speaking to me and calling me into His service too. I wonder how many times God has used these same Scriptures down through the years to call other men and women into His service?

Whenever God gives us a personal word, it is anointed and there is power in it. I have found whenever you return to that word, it continues to encourage and strengthen you. I have returned to those words many times through the years. Each time they would encourage and strengthen me, and they still do today.

What I finally came to see was that Joshua was Old Covenant, and Paul was New Covenant. Joshua was functioning under the Law, and Paul was functioning under grace and faith. Before Paul met the Lord Jesus, he was under the law too. But after he met Jesus, he functioned under grace and faith. I now believe that all of us go through this same transition.

Many of us are brought up in a Christian church where we learn the laws, rules, and regulations. We learn the rituals and traditions just like the Jews did, just like Paul did, and we serve the letter of the law.

At some point in our lifetime, we reach out to God with all of our heart, with all of our strength, with everything within us, and we break through the veil and touch the living God. We are never the same again. We are not called to serve the letter of the law anymore. Now we are called to serve the Spirit of the law of life in Christ Jesus. These laws are now written in the tablets of our heart, day by day.

When I encountered Jesus and the living Word, I then had a problem with the church. I saw that many of the traditions and laws of the church were man-made and that some people were in bondage to these man-made laws. People did not obey these laws because they loved God, but because they feared God.

I remember as a child growing up that I had to go to church, and I didn't like it at all. I was bored; it lasted too long and I couldn't wait to get out. Now I see the church in a totally different way. I want to go. I enjoy going; it is not a prison anymore.

The church is an institution made up of a set of laws, rules, regulations, rituals and traditions. But the same church as the spiritual body of Christ does not function under a set of laws or rules and regulations; it is led by the Holy Spirit and functions through grace and faith.

The church is difficult to understand. It seems that if I just accept the church without any questions, just in obedience, and do what I am told or taught—no problem. But as soon as I begin to question what the church is all about, things begin to get complicated.

The law has two aspects: the letter that kills, and the Spirit that gives life. A wonderful example of this is the Israelites and the Samaritan. They both believed in God but their approach was different. You can see this difference in the parable of the Good Samaritan. The priest and the Levite went to the other side of the road and offered no help; the Samaritan went right to the injured man and helped him.

The priest and the Levite were under the letter of the law, and the Samaritan functioning in the Spirit of the law. The priest and Levite were bound by the law, but the Samaritan was fulfilling the law.

53

Faith and the Power of God

My family is Catholic, and I was brought up in the Catholic faith. If you had asked me, "Do you believe in God?" I would have had to say, "Yes!" If you asked, "Do you believe in Jesus Christ and the Holy Spirit?" again I would have to say, "Yes I think so."

But if you would have asked me, "Do you know God? Do you know Jesus Christ? Do you know the Holy Spirit?" I would have had to say, "No, I do not know them; I only believe they are there."

I want to make this clear. The Catholic church instilled in me a belief or a faith that there was a God. He heard prayers, He sometimes answered them with a miracle or healing, and He watched over us.

The church also instilled in me the belief that Jesus Christ died for my sins, that He sent back the Holy Spirit to help us and to guide us, and that we could call on Him anytime we needed to. Another important truth it taught me was that I was a sinner.

I thank God for the church and for what it did for me, instilling in me a faith in God, Jesus Christ and the Holy Spirit. This faith was a blessing to me for many years as I grew up and wandered all over the country; when I went into the Marine Corps and was in the Korean war; when I came back and did some more wandering; and then when I married Pauline at age twenty-five.

But seven years after we married, my faith did not seem to be enough to save our marriage. At that point some wonderful things began to happen in my life. The best way I can describe it is with a Scripture from 1 Corinthians 2:5:

> *... that your faith should not rest on the wisdom of men, but on the power of God.*

I had an electrical business, and I did a lot of service work. One day I was working in a crawl space and I had to climb over a bunch of cables and pipes. One of the cables was not grounded properly, and I received a very bad electric shock from my left shoulder down to my left hip. This stunned me in some way.

When I came to, I was out of the crawl space and walking around in circles in the basement. My body felt funny and shaky all over. I sat down for a few minutes and then was able to go back to work.

But the next day something happened that scared me. I was going up some stairs and my heart acted real strange. There was no pain, but something was wrong with my heart. I realized that the electrical shock had gone right through my heart and did something to it. My heart would beat real fast and not very even. After a few minutes, it would level out again.

From that day on, it began to happen more frequently, like every few days. We did not have any insurance. I didn't want to tell Pauline and frighten her, but I knew the problem was getting worse.

There was a man and wife from England having some healing services in the area. One night we went to their healing service. There were about forty people there, and we were all sitting in a circle singing some Christian songs.

Suddenly something happened to me: it was like a large glass container came down over me and closed me off from everyone. People were talking and singing, but I could not hear them. Then all feeling of weight left me; it was like I was floating above the floor.

The next thing that happened was the most amazing of all. I felt a hand form right inside my chest; I could feel it there so clearly. Then it moved up to my heart and held it. A very clear thought came into my mind: "Your heart is healed."

The hand just faded out and was gone. The feeling of weight came back. This thing that had been around me lifted up and was gone, and I knew I was healed. I never had any more problems with my heart.

I remembered the Scripture in 1 Corinthians 2:5, "that your faith should not rest on the wisdom of men, but on the power of God."

Pauline and I have had many of these wonderful experiences of the power of God. The next one happened to Pauline. She was very sick and had gone to the doctor. The report was not good. She had a large mass in the area of her female organs, as large as a grapefruit, and she was in a lot of pain.

The doctor told her she needed to go to the hospital right away and have an operation. But first she needed medication to clear the infection, before they could operate. So Pauline asked if she could go home and take the medication there, instead of in the hospital. The doctor didn't really want to, but he allowed her to do that. She was to go to the hospital at the end of the week.

Two days later, there was a prayer meeting in the area, and Pauline was determined to go even though she was very sick. She asked for prayer and the laying on of hands for healing. The group gathered around her, laid hands on her, and prayed for healing. The Spirit of God came on her, and she was slain in the Spirit. She would have fallen out of the chair, if we were not holding her. At the same time, the Lord spoke to me and said, "She is healed!" When she came to, we went home.

For the next three days she was very sick and could not get out of bed. On the fourth day, she rushed to the bathroom and all kinds of stuff drained out of her. The following day she had to go back to the doctor before she checked into the hospital. The doctor was amazed, because the poison was all gone. The hard, woody growth had shrunk to the size of a walnut. The doctor sent her home and had her come back a week later, and this mass was all gone.

> *... that your faith should not rest on the wisdom of men, but on the power of God.*

I can only go by my experiences, but it seems that my faith has changed from what I had as a young man. I believed because of what I was taught and told by others, but I had not experienced the power of God myself, so my faith was very shaky at times.

Now my faith rests on these powerful things that God has done for me and my family, and I know it is much stronger than it was then.

There are two levels of faith: one based on the wisdom and teaching of others, the other on the power of God itself. The question for all of us is: what is our faith based on? The wisdom of men? Or the power of God?

54

Institutions

Often when the Lord has something to say to me, it is when I first wake up in the morning. I like to lie still and be aware of God's presence in me and with me. One morning the Holy Spirit spoke to me about "institutions." He was showing me that the church is both a spiritual organism with Christ as its head, and an institution, comprised of laws, rules, regulations, rituals and traditions.

Later I looked up the word "institution" in the dictionary. I don't want to explain all that this word means. You can look it up if you care to, but there are certain aspects of its meaning I thought were interesting. One of the meanings of institution is establishment; there must be rules and regulations established.

The word "institutionalism" was also interesting. It places an emphasis on organization, as in religion, at the expense of other factors. Public institutionalism referred to the care of defective, delinquent or dependant persons. I thought that was interesting too—the care of defective, delinquent or dependent persons. I expect some church people might be insulted by that description.

When we start being institutionalized, we begin to lose touch with the Holy Spirit. Why is it that, if we allow ourselves to be institutionalized in a church, we lose touch with the Holy Spirit? It is because we go back to a set of rules and regulations that have no power, instead of being led by the Holy Spirit. This is what happened to the foolish Galatians.

Several times in the past years I have seen groups of people meeting in homes or halls, praying together, studying together, and the Holy Spirit working mightily in their midst. Someone would come up with the idea that they should form a church, and they did! But soon afterwards, most of the gifts of the Holy Spirit ceased, and they were not manifested any more.

Why did the manifestations cease? As soon as you begin to be institutionalized, you are once more submitting yourself to the letter of the law, not the Spirit of the law.

We do need the organized church. It is an instrument, a platform, from which we can reach out to the world, preaching the gospel and meeting the needs of people in a way we never could individually. But God never intended the church to be a prison or to control us.

I believe the best description of the institutional church is described in Galatians 3:23-24:

> *But before faith came, we were kept in custody under the law, being shut up to the faith which was later to be revealed. Therefore the law has become our tutor to lead us to Christ, that we might be justified by faith.*

The church as an institution or an establishment is a law system to preach Christ.

> *But now that faith has come you are no longer under a tutor. (Galatians 3:25)*

Once faith comes, we are not to be led by the church; we are to be led by the Spirit.

> *... who also made us adequate as servants of a new covenant, not of the letter, but of the Spirit; for the letter kills, but the Spirit gives life. (2 Corinthians 3:6)*

As soon as we allow religious institutions to direct our life, we start coming under the influence of the letter of the law and we lose the freedom that is in the Spirit of the law. The Holy Spirit works by the Spirit of the law, not the letter. In Galatians, it says:.

> *Are you so foolish? Having begun by the Spirit, are you now being perfected by the flesh? (Galatians 3:3)*

Does He then, who provides you with the Spirit and works miracles among you, do it by the works of the Law, or by hearing with faith? (Galatians 3:5)

Understand this! We can work in the church, be involved in the church, and still enjoy the freedom that is in Christ. Do not allow yourself to be institutionalized by the church. Don't become one of the foolish Galatians. Don't fall back under the letter of the law that kills; be led by the Spirit.

Beware, if you have not had a born-again experience and do not know the Holy Spirit or know how to be led by the Holy Spirit. You need the church and its laws to guide and direct you until you experience these foundational building blocks. Otherwise you would be a lawless person and you would not have any protection against our enemy, Satan.

55

Wine Skins

When I experienced the Lord in a deeper spiritual way, I had some very interesting things begin to occur in my religious life. I became much more active in my local church, and I wanted the local church to become more active in spiritual things. To my amazement, they weren't interested in my spirituality and did not care about becoming more spiritual themselves.

I began to go to church every day. The church was not full—there were only about five people there on a daily basis—but the church was full on Saturday evening and Sunday morning. Every week they were announcing a need for readers at the Sunday services and a need for people to teach the children CCD on Saturday mornings. I volunteered to read at the services, and Pauline and I volunteered to teach CCD. Our desire was to see these children come to a closer walk with Jesus, but I never expected what happened next.

After several weeks went by, we were told that we were not needed anymore. The pastor was a fine man and very gently told us that the parents of these students complained we talked about Jesus too much, so they did not want us to teach them. They also complained about my reading at the services, and that I could not do that anymore. All I was doing was reading the weekly Scriptures. To say the least, I was a little upset over all this, because I thought that in the church we were to speak of Jesus, and in CCD to teach our kids about Jesus.

I might have left the church at that time, but the pastor encouraged me to stay and also the Holy Spirit told me I was to stay. Then the Holy Spirit led me to Matthew 9:16-17:

> *"But no one puts a patch of unshrunk cloth on an old garment; for the patch pulls away from the garment, and a worse tear results.*

Nor do men put new wine into old wineskins; otherwise the wineskins burst, and the wine pours out, and the wineskins are ruined; but they put new wine into fresh wineskins, and both are preserved."

I realized the Lord was showing me an important truth regarding the church. If we tried to force our new experience with Jesus and the Holy Spirit on these people, who had become rigid in their faith and could not receive anything new, it could bring division and divide the church.

I could see that God had set me free in a new and wonderful way, but I could not force that freedom onto others. I had tasted the new wine and enjoyed it, and we wanted everyone in our church to enjoy it also, but it was not to be. When you put new wine that is still working into an old wineskin which has become hard and set, it breaks the old wineskin and all is lost.

Old wine can be very good, but it has ceased working; it is not changing anymore like new wine is. When we see this truth, we can enjoy the new wine and the old wine.

New wine is put into new wine skins, so the skins can stretch as the wine is working. When it stops working, the skin hardens and becomes brittle. The church is similar; a new church is flexible, but as the years go by, it becomes more and more inflexible. This has happened to all the churches. When we become aware of this principle, we can stop trying to change these churches and as a result there are not so many church divisions.

Churches that understand this truth learn how to deal with the new wine and the old wine, without causing dissension in the church. Perhaps they have a very ritualistic, traditional Sunday morning service. Then the Sunday evening service has a lot more flexibility, a time for people to share testimonies, pray over one another, and use the gifts of the Holy Spirit.

Some churches have midweek prayer meetings, where folks have freedom to praise God, sing in the Spirit, and use the gifts of the Holy Spirit. People can partake of the old wine and the new wine and enjoy both—without breaking the old wineskin.

56

Two or More

When I was a kid I did not like school very well; now I realize why. I was a very active little boy, and my attention span was very short. Today they would have a name for this type of thing: attention deficit disorder.

Well, this behavior carried right along to my church experiences too. As far as I was concerned, church lasted too long. This also affected my Saturday mornings. This was my day off from school and I wanted to play, but I was sent off to catechism for the morning.

At the time I didn't know what an important impact these things would have on my life. I was retaining some good things from them. At school I was learning to read and write and how to function with other people about my age. In church and catechism, I was learning some things about God, and faith in God was entering into my heart and soul. I now look back and say, "Thank God for the blessing from these things that I was made to do."

I still have this short attention problem today, but I now know how to deal with it. I keep several projects going at the same time, and I shift from one project to another whenever I reach the end of my attention span.

Pauline and I spend a lot of time together at home and when we are on the road traveling. We do not talk a lot; I drive and Pauline reads. From time to time, we pray for people who are in need and for the meeting that we are going to do. It is a time of peace and quiet and the Lord speaks to me a lot during this time. I also spend a lot of this time just enjoying His presence and talking with Him. It is a very pleasant time for the three of us: the Lord, Pauline, and me.

"Again I say to you, that if two of you agree on earth about anything that they may ask, it shall be done for them by My Father who is in heaven. For where two or three have gathered together in My name, I am there in their midst." (Matthew 18:19-20)

Many times when we are having dinner at home or in a restaurant, we talk about the Lord and pray for someone in the church or family or for other prayer needs we know of. We get into some really good spiritual discussions and talk about our faith and what we believe. I learn some really good things and get to share some good things as well.

... and let us consider how to stimulate one another to love and good deeds, not forsaking our own assembling together, as is the habit of some, but encouraging one another; and all the more as you see the day drawing near. (Hebrews 10:24-25)

Often I hear these Scriptures in Hebrews used in regard to attending our church assembly. This is certainly a part of what they are referring to, but they are also referring to our getting together everyday, praying with each other, and sharing our faith one on one, when we are apart from the church assembly. We need to stimulate one another often, seven days a week, in our play, our home life and our work life. Without this we all suffer loss.

We need to get together often with believers and nonbelievers and not be afraid to share our Christian faith. Do not be intimidated by nonbelievers. Some people do not talk about Jesus and their faith in their own home, because there is a nonbeliever there. This is a very good reason to share our faith so they can become believers.

I have often asked the question: have any of you ever received a healing or miracle? Most every hand goes up, every time. This is what we all need to share, "Jesus gave me a miracle. Jesus healed me of this affliction and set me free."

Where two or three of us come together in His name, miracles, healings and all kinds of wonderful things do happen. Many of these healings and miracles do not happen at a church meeting or a healing service, but they happen when two or three people simply pray for one another on the street, in a restaurant, or in a home.

We must believe that He is there, and we must expect good things are going to happen because He is there. There doesn't have to be a priest or pastor, an evangelist, or a miracle worker present. Jesus is there; the Holy Spirit is there. That is all we need.

These people in ministry are just like you and me; we all have the same relationship with Jesus. We need to respect those in positions of leadership, but we are not to elevate them. We are all sinners who have been forgiven.

We need to be an expectant people. It is so easy to become complacent. If you have a big-name healer come to your church, you go there expecting something to happen. But what about at every Sunday service? Do you expect something to happen there? Why not?

Do we need to be expectant when two or three come together in Jesus' name for a prayer time, at a coffee time, or for a meal in a restaurant? Certainly!

We have had some of the most wonderful times sitting in restaurants talking about Jesus, sharing our dreams and visions, our healings and miracles. Then, suddenly we would realize that all the people around us were listening to what we were sharing. We recognized that Jesus was reaching out to the people around us while we shared.

Don't restrict your Christian influence to a few hours a week in church or the mid-week service. Keep it active at all times, especially in your home, and when you are with two or more other believers in Jesus Christ.

57

The Brass Heaven

When we speak of a brass heaven, it means our prayers are not getting through. When I was in the service working around aviation fuel, we used brass tools because brass does not give off a spark. To reach God, we need a spark; faith is our spark that reaches God's throne.

It seems at times that God is not listening, so the question we have is: Is He hearing me? Or sometimes we hear the phrase "Is anybody there?"

From what I know of God our Father, the Bible says He knows our very thoughts before we even ask. I believe this to be true! I think He has heard every prayer I've ever uttered, even when it was misdirected. Now I thank God that He didn't answer most of them. But what I believe is not important; it is what you believe that is important.

There are many reasons why prayer is not answered, but when a prayer is not answered that doesn't mean it is not heard by God. He may be answering differently than you expected. The answer to your prayer may be harmful in ways you don't understand. There are times when our prayers do more harm than good. Other times, we are praying for things that are harmful to us.

Sometimes God is waiting for something to change in our life before our prayers are answered. Has God been nudging you over and over about some issue in your life, and you have been ignoring Him?

I remember several years of my life, when it seemed God was not hearing or answering my prayers. When He finally answered my prayers, I asked Him why He didn't answer them quicker. He answered, "Because your prayers were not big enough." God wanted to answer my prayers. He wants to answer yours. It might be wise to ask God why He is not answering your prayers.

I no longer pray for as many things as I used to pray for. Now I know most all of those things He is going to provide anyway at the right time.

Another trouble spot seems to be when God has already given us clear direction in some area of our life and we have not followed through and accomplished it. We continue to keep asking for more direction and we hear nothing more. We would like the whole plan laid out ahead of us, but you know what? He is not going to do it! When I stop hearing directions from God, I had better look back and pay attention to what He told me to do last and get about doing it.

Another major problem is our sick attitude, thinking we can boss God around and tell Him just what to do. I am so spiritual and have so much faith to move mountains that God has to do just what I tell him to do. A proper label for this is spiritual pride; this is what got Satan in trouble.

Beware, sometimes God gives you just what you want if you really demand it. The Israelites demanded a king when God had appointed judges over them. He gave them a king and told them that they and their sons and daughters will have to serve the king.

When you demand something from God, and He gives it to you, you will land up serving it—whatever it is. One thing I have learned: give everything you have to God and just be a caretaker. Then you truly become free. After a while we learn that everything we own, owns *us*!

58

Spiritual Beings

We are body, soul and spirit. Most of us are very aware of our physical body and its needs. The same is true with our soul, comprised of our mind, emotions, and all the abilities we have to function in this world and with one another. Most of us know very little about our spirit and other spirits.

A spirit has ability to think and reason, and it has emotions. There are other spirits in this world that do not have a physical body or a soul. These spirits desire a body to live in, and they will live in yours if you do not guard it. Many people already have another spirit living in them, and some have several; for the most part, they are not even aware of it.

Some people are very afraid of spirits. Others are aware of them, and even entertain them and communicate with them and welcome them into their life—not a good idea unless it is the Holy Spirit.

Spirits for the most part are invisible, but some can appear as people at times. They can also appear as animals or birds. God is spirit, and the Bible is the best source of information about spirits and the many kinds of spirits there are.

There are many spirits in this world, but because they are not visible to the eye, we are not very aware of them. They can torment your mind and cause turmoil in your home. Many of the sicknesses have a spiritual root. Jesus cast them out; we do not. We take pills and drugs, and wonder why we are not healed.

I do not consider myself an expert in this field, but in forty-five years of helping people with spiritual problems, I have learned a lot.

Spirit of Infirmity

Many of our sicknesses have a spiritual root or are spirits that have inhabited our bodies or our soul. Fear and worry are the open door for some of these spiritual things to enter in. I believe fear is what allows many spiritual infirmities to become active in our bodies.

We have seen numbers of people with arthritis and other related infirmities totally freed. Using the authority God has given us, through the name of Jesus Christ, we command the infirmities to leave the body. I know many people have tried this with no results.

To use this authority you must have received Jesus Christ as your Lord and have been baptized in the Holy Spirit. You must also believe that you have the authority over evil spirits. If you do not have the authority from the Holy Spirit, do not try to cast these spirits out; you may land up with the spirit yourself.

If you understand there are spiritual infirmaries that affect your physical body, then you realize why doctors, medicine, and drugs cannot heal everyone. If the spirit of infirmity is driven out first, then these other methods can bring healing.

Spiritual infirmities do not always leave instantly, although sometimes they do. They might leave the person in an hour or two, sometimes in a day or two. They must leave when handled with authority. They can damage the body, so that it takes time for the body to heal. There are miracles, and the body or soul is healed instantly.

These spiritual beings are very interested in people. They want to destroy, inhabit or use you. Satan and one third of the angels were cast out of Heaven. Earth is their prison and, as I understand it, they cannot leave. They do not die like we do; they continually move from one person to another as they can find someone open.

Jesus Defeated Spiritual Powers

Jesus Christ came into this world so that you and I could be free from the power of sin and be restored in our relationship to God. Jesus came to set the captives free. He came to destroy the works of the devil.

> *For our struggle is not against flesh and blood, but against the rulers, against the powers, against the world forces of this darkness, against the spiritual forces of wickedness in the heavenly places. (Ephesians 6:12)*

Jesus Christ defeated these spiritual powers; He also gave us everything we need to defeat them. If they can keep you in darkness, ignorant of how they work, they have the victory.

There are those who believe that when they die, they are just born again, becoming another person; each time they die they are becoming a more perfect person. If this were true there should be a few perfect people around, but there aren't.

Several years ago there was big story about a woman; I believe her name was Bridy Murphy. This woman remembered things that happened to her several generations back. She knew names, events, all kinds of things you would not know unless you were there.

Many of the things she talked about and described proved to be right on. Was this proof that indeed we just die and become another person? No! It only proved she had another spirit, not hers, but another spirit that had known many people down through the years.

When these spirits, which I call a familiar spirits, live with a person, they know all about them. These spirits know who your friends are. They know all your habits and your sins. They even know your language and remember all these things. When you die this spirit moves on to another body.

In most if not all of these cases, the host person is never aware a familiar spirit is living right in them. Don't be taken in by those who claim they are going to live over and over again.

And inasmuch as it is appointed for men to die once and after this comes judgment. (Hebrews 9:27)

I want to encourage you to use the spiritual senses you have. Just be still and try to sense the spirits around you; in your home, in your workplace, and in the people around you. You may be surprised at the discernment of spirits you already have, if you will only use the ability.

59

Window of The Soul

Our eyes are the window of our soul. They reveal many things we do not want others to know. Mothers seem to know this truth, and many times they can tell when the children are lying because their eyes give them away. When we have a problem in our soul, it can be very difficult for us to look another person in the eye.

When we have one of these spiritual beings living in us, they look out through our eyes. This is a problem for them because, if there is someone around with discernment, they can be seen for what they are. They will turn away and not look you in the eye; they do not want to be seen.

If you have a problem looking people in the eye, ask yourself a question, "Why do I have this problem? Is there something in me that wants to remain hidden? What is it?"

Sometimes it is because I am ashamed, or am guilty, or am hiding something. If that is the issue then deal with it before it makes you sick. If you recognize it as a spirit of some kind, go to someone who can set you free from it. It is nothing to be ashamed of, and you don't have to continue to live with that spirit or protect it. You can be sure it is robbing you of something.

These spiritual being are like leeches. They take away your health, your peace and joy. They even rob you of your friends. They lead you into the darkness instead of the light.

Try looking into people's eyes and really pay attention to what you see. You will see all kinds of things. You will see love and peace; you will see anger and distrust; and now and then you will see an evil spirit looking out at you.

When you look in some people's eyes, it is like a dark hole, as if there is no soul there. These people have no conscience. They are very dangerous and they do not value life. These people are full of evil spiritual beings.

Religious Spirits

One of the methods these spiritual things take advantage of is religion. Many of these spirits are religious spirits and are involved in religions around the world. I expect most of you are aware that religion is dangerous. It has been instrumental in killing and murdering millions of people in the world and is still doing it.

Religious spirits are very common—there are many throughout the church and the religions of the world. These spirits can be recognized in that they are enemies of Jesus Christ and the Holy Spirit. They may use the name of Jesus and speak about the Holy Spirit, but they don't believe in a born-again or conversion experience or in being baptized in the Holy Spirit.

These spirits lock people in religious practices, causing these folks to try and perfect themselves instead of turning to Jesus. One of the dangers is that some of these people are in positions of leadership. They do not enter into a relationship with Jesus Christ and the Holy Spirit, and they hinder others from entering in as well.

Religious spirits are very dangerous; Satan has used these spirits to cause many wars down through the years. They are still causing wars and killing people today. If you don't agree with their doctrine and submit to it, they kill you. These spirits can kill you with guns and weapons, and they can also kill you with words.

Spirits are deadly in another way; they can convince you through the practice of religion that you are right with God when you have no relationship with Him at all. They cause the church to be the center of your attention rather than Jesus Christ.

Religious spirits are very legalistic and contentious. They like to argue over doctrine and religious practices, but they do not have a testimony of God's power working in their life. These spirits will try to confound you with questions you can not answer.

They will also use Scriptures to confuse you. They will preach another Jesus with a watered down gospel and without the cross. They will claim that Jesus was only a prophet and not the son Of God.

These deceiving religious spirits will try to convince you that there are many ways to God. That is a lie. There is only one way to God, and that is through Jesus Christ and the cross. Without the blood of the Lamb there is no forgiveness of sin; all that awaits us is judgment.

Spirit of Suicide

Many people take their own lives; we choose to call it suicide. The truth is some of these people are murdered. It can be a deliberate car accident, a hanging, cutting a blood vessel, jumping from a tall building, or jumping from a bridge into a river to drown. The Scriptures speak about some of these methods spirits use to murder people.

These spirits affect our emotions and our thinking; these lying, deceiving spirits depress our emotions and fill our minds with lying thoughts. When this happens, we think these emotions and thoughts are our own; they are not. The enemy is at work laying groundwork to take your life or cause you to take someone else's life.

In many cases (prescription) drugs are tried, and they do help to save some people. The problem is that the spirits involved are still there, and as soon as a person is off the drugs, the spirit is active again to kill them. In other cases the drugs themselves leave the open door for spirits to enter in.

You see, spirits want to kill others as well as the person they inhabit; these spirits come to murder, kill and destroy whoever they can. They do not respect persons; you can be a doctor, lawyer, counselor, priest, or minister. There is only one thing they recognize: the authority that is in the name of Jesus Christ.

I bear witness that these murderous spirits are on this earth, always looking for another target to use and abuse. We have seen a four-year-old child wanting to kill himself. We have sat at a table with a man and his wife and children eating dinner when this man jumps up, grabs a large knife, and is going to kill himself.

I have had to chase a man and tackle him to the ground; he was going to jump into a swollen river and drown himself. We have had a large man stand two feet in front of us, spitting and growling like an animal, telling us he was going to kill us. These were people being controlled by an evil spirit.

Very few Christian people know how to handle or cope with these situations. The whole church is sadly lacking in knowledge of how to deal with these situations. Many people are afraid to even learn about this subject.

We do not have to be afraid of spirits. If we have the knowledge and understanding, and know who we are in Christ, these spirits are afraid of us.

My people are destroyed for lack of knowledge ... (Hosea 4:6)

I thought the following Scripture fits in very well for this day and age:

Therefore My people go into exile for their lack of knowledge, and their honorable men are famished, and their multitude is parched with thirst. Therefore Sheol has enlarged its throat and opened its mouth without measure. (Isaiah 5:13-14)

Seducing Spirits

Seducing spirits. The spirit of seduction has done great harm to the church and to the family. Seldom is it recognized for what it is: an evil spirit. This spirit has destroyed many priest and ministers as well as husbands and wives. These spirits destroy our well-being and self-worth.

The *Merriam-Webster Dictionary* describes seduce in this way:

Seduce: 1) to persuade to disobedience or disloyalty; 2) to lead astray; 3) to entice to unlawful sexual intercourse without the use of force (syn: tempt, entice, inveigle, lure – seducer —seduction—seductive).

The spirit of seduction is very tricky; it works through our natural desires for love and affection, and we don't even see it for what it is. We think it is our own desires wanting to be fulfilled, but it is not. Some people have the spirit of seduction *in* them; others have a spirit of seduction *with* them.

Another interesting thing about these types of spirits is that they may not have any effect on the person who carries them or they are attached to; instead they affect the people around them. Another aspect of these spirits is that they are promiscuous; they are not happy with one partner. They do not love; they simply desire sex and related activity with numerous people of various sexes, including animals.

Like many of the other spirits, they seem to know our weak areas. They prey especially on the fleshly desires and our thoughts and emotions. Like all other spirits, they are deceivers; they have been around a long time and have misled many people. Thank God through Jesus Christ we can recognize these spirits and be freed from them.

Seducing spirits work against God's people in another way:

" … for false Christs and false prophets will arise, and will show signs and wonders, in order, if possible, to lead the elect astray." (Mark 13:22)

But evil men and imposters will proceed from bad to worse, deceiving and being deceived. (2 Timothy 3:13)

But the Spirit explicitly says that in the later times some will fall away from the faith, paying attention to deceitful spirits and doctrines of demons. (1 Timothy 4 :1)

Be aware! There are spirits that want to seduce you. We have men and women that also enjoy seducing others. We also have religions and churches that desire to seduce you and bring you under their control. Be wise and do not let yourself be seduced by any of these things.

Home Spirits

One of the interesting spirits we have encountered in our spiritual journey is what I would call "home spirits." The reason I call them home spirits is because they inhabit homes. It seems as if quite a number of homes have their own spirit of one kind or another.

The spirits revel themselves in several different ways. I wouldn't label these spirits good or bad, they could be either.

In some of these homes the folks that live there are aware of them. They even see them from time to time, but this doesn't seem to bother them too much and they simple ignore them. Most people call them ghosts; they are just spirits wandering around. As strange as it seems, spirits get lonely. They like to be around people; they like a home, and they seem to like a home life.

Some people that have good spiritual sight can see these spirits and communicate with them. Some of these home-loving spirits can move objects and touch people. These spirits are a lot like people in that they can become very attached to objects; if you move the object, they get very disturbed. They may live in the same home for generations.

Years ago when I was an electrician, I was working in this old farmhouse where several families were living together like a commune. They were all gone for several days to some celebration. I was working along doing my wiring job and a little thought kept entering my mind. "I am lonely."

This thought occurred several times. I finally realized it was not my thought; a spirit was speaking to me. I spoke out loud and asked, "Why are you lonely?" It answered, "My family is all gone and I am lonely."

As I was thinking about this, I realized this spirit considered these folks to be its family, and when they were gone for any reason, this spirit missed them. I expect many of these other home spirits are very attached to the families that live in these homes.

Both demons and angels are spirits. We have good spirits and evil spirits. The Bible tells us to test every spirit. God give us the discernment to know the difference so as not to be deceived by them.

60

The Holy Spirit Helps Us

God is spirit. Jesus is spirit, but He also had a body and soul, having been born a man. Man is also spirit, but many people are spiritually dead and need a born-again experience.

Spiritual beings have a mind and emotions just like the natural man has. There is an interesting Scripture in Revelation 1:4:

> *John, to the seven churches that are in Asia: Grace to you and peace, from Him who is and who was and who is the come; and from the seven Spirits who are before His throne; and from Jesus Christ, the faithful witness, the first born of the dead, and the ruler of the kings of the earth. To Him who loves us, and released us from our sins by His blood.*

I just wanted you to notice that in this salutation there was a distinction between Him, the seven Spirits, and Jesus Christ.

In Isaiah 11:1-2 it says:

> *Then a shoot will spring from the stem of Jesse, and a branch from his roots will bear fruit. And the Spirit of the Lord will rest on him, the spirit of wisdom and understanding, the spirit of counsel and strength, the spirit of knowledge and the fear of the Lord.*

This Scripture has to be referring to Jesus; these spirits were going to rest on Him. This very much sounds like the gifts of the Holy Spirit, the very same spirits that come with the baptism of the Holy Spirit.

We are not left helpless in a world full of strange spirits. We have the Holy Spirit and a multitude of angels watching over us. They have intervened in our lives many times when we were totally unaware of them.

> *And after being baptized, Jesus went up immediately from the water; and behold, the heavens were opened, and he saw the Spirit of God descending as a dove, and coming upon Him. (Matthew 3:16)*

This was at the time that Jesus began His work and ministry; healing the sick and setting the demon possessed free.

This same Holy Spirit comes to us when we ask, heals us and sets us free. We are then capable to help others to function properly in the spiritual realm.

It is important to learn as much as we can about these spirits so that we can recognize the spirits that want to do us harm and the spirits that are here to help us. Through Jesus Christ, our Father in heaven has given us authority over these evil spirits. We must recognize them and know how to use this God-given authority to defeat them.

Spiritually Aware

If you are ever going to come to a place of spiritual growth and maturity and continue on in your spiritual journey and truly be led by the Holy Spirit, there are certain truths you must understand. They are set forth in the following teaching St. Paul gave to the Corinthians.

> *... but just as it is written, "Things which eye has not seen and ear has not heard, and which have not entered the heart of man, all that God has prepared for those who love Him."*
>
> *For to us God revealed them through the Spirit; for the Spirit searches all things, even the depths of God. For who among men know the thoughts of a man except the spirit of the man, which is in him? Even so the thoughts of God no one knows except the Spirit of God.*
>
> *Now we have received, not the spirit of the world, but the Spirit who is from God, that we might know the things freely given to us by God, which things we also speak, not in words taught by human wisdom, but in those taught by the Spirit, combining spiritual thoughts with spiritual words.*
>
> *But a natural man does not accept the things of the Spirit of God; for they are foolishness to him, and he cannot understand them, because they are spiritually appraised. But he who is spiritual appraises all things, yet he himself is appraised by no man.*
>
> *For Who has known the mind of the Lord, that he should instruct Him? But we have the mind of Christ. (1 Corinthians 2:9-16)*

I could try going from one Scripture to another explaining what I think they mean. You might even get some understanding in your natural mind. This would not help you at all because this is a spiritual message intended for your spirit. Our spirit is the only one who has the capability to understand this teaching.

I encourage all of you to spend some time pondering this wonderful teaching from Paul until you get the revelation in your spirit of what the Holy Spirit wants you to understand.

Seeing With Spiritual Eyes

Animals can also be troubled by spirits. We have come in contact with these spirits numerous times. I have laid hands on and prayed for sick animals and had great results. Cows, dogs, birds and horses have all responded well to prayer.

Some of these animals were possessed by a spirits; they acted real crazy. They were mean and dangerous, but after taking authority over the spirits and commanding them to leave, they were okay.

We did prayer and healing meetings in homes. I always learned to keep my eye on the pet dogs and cats. If they had a spirit, they would go nuts, scratching and spitting and racing around the room. They would have to put the pets in another room.

When there are spirits around, they sometimes appear as animals. One person had a lot of pain in their chest and had a spiritual bear hugging them. When we commanded the bear to leave, the pain was gone. Another person was having a problem with their back; a large spiritual monkey was sitting on his back. One lady was very sick to her stomach, and a thing that looked like an small owl was sitting on her arm. When we rebuked it, she ran into the bathroom, threw up, and was fine.

These spirits can also appear in other ways. One man was having terrible headaches; this spirit looked like a large boring tool right down into the top of his head. I asked the Lord what to do about it, and He told me to just reach up, grab it, and turn it out. I did that. The man fell to the floor, and a few minutes later when he got up the headache was gone.

One lady was having terrible cramps in the lower part of her leg. I could see something like a torture instrument attached to her leg. The lord told me to pull it off; I did. Her leg cramps were gone.

I don't pretend to understand some of these things; with spiritual eyes we can see some of these spirits. With spiritual hearing we receive directions from the Holy Spirit and know how to deal with them

Learn as much as you can about spirits and spiritual things so that you can deal with them if they become active in your home. We do not have to be afraid of them. We do need to be knowledgeable. The best instructor we have concerning spirits is the Holy Spirit.

The Human Spirit

One more spirit it is important to speak of; each one of us has a spirit. In some folks their spirit is very active. In other folks their spirit is very inactive—if there is any activity at all.

The Bible tells us that before we are born-again we are dead in our trespasses and sin. This is probably referring to our spirit, because the body and soul is active enough. It could be referring to the fact that we are dead to God's spirit. I say this because some people seem to be active spiritually to other spirits; they have not had a born-again experience with the Holy Spirit.

The Bible tells us to test every spirit; this would include our spirit and the spirit of other people. Some people seem very spiritual, and they are; but their spirit is filled with darkness, not light. These folks are not in touch with the Holy Spirit; they are in touch with other spirits that appear as angels of light—deceiving spirits.

The Bible also tells us you shall "know them by their fruit," not by their gifts or callings. What fruit? The fruit of the Holy Spirit is love, joy, peace, faith, and righteousness. This is what should be in our spirit.

Our spirit can have several problems. We can have a broken spirit. We can have a weak spirit. All of our emotions—fear, sadness, sorrow, grief, and others—can affect our spirit. We can also have a bitter, angry, hateful spirit. If this is the case, you are a difficult person to be around.

Another problem arises when we are not functioning well, so we think an evil spirit has entered in, and we try to cast it out. We cannot cast out an evil spirit if it is our own spirit. Nobody else can cast it out either.

A different situation arises when our spirit begins to develop. It wants to rise up into the leadership position it was created for. The lower nature of the soul which has been in control doesn't want to relinquish that control. We have a power struggle between the spirit and the soul.

St. Paul speaks about the natural man and the spiritual man. When the natural man takes control, people suffer defeats and fall back into their old ways. When the spirit is in control, the Christian person has some wonderful victories.

Part Six

Discovering More Light

61

Questions and Answers

Questions are very important. Our lives are filled with them from the time of our childhood. Kids ask the strangest questions, like the one my grandson asked his mother one day when he was sitting on the pot: “Why does Jesus want to live inside of us when we stink so badly?”

Most of our children are full of questions. Some of these questions are very profound and some of them seem very foolish. Some of them are hard to answer, while others have no answers.

When children start school, the teachers explain and teach them many things, but now the children have to start answering questions. The older they get, the more complex the questions.

One of the programs I like to watch on television is Charlie Rose. The reason I enjoy the program is because he interviews people from all kinds of backgrounds and knows how to ask questions. Asking the right question is important.

I have another friend, Judy Doctor, who also knows how to ask questions. If we know how to ask the right questions and we are willing to look for the answer or to look at the answer, it can bring us into a new place—and it has the power to change our lives.

Many the times down through the years I have asked the Lord questions. Instead of giving me an answer, He would ask me a question in return. You can give someone all the right answers, but it doesn’t help them at all. For example, you can give a student all the right answers to pass a test, but they are no smarter than they were before.

I came to the place where I began to wait for the next question from the Lord, because I knew that He wanted me to see something and understand something new.

A great many times in the ministry, people would come to Pauline and me looking for an answer to something. We knew what the answer was, but the answer would not have helped them. All the Lord had for them was a question—He wanted them to find the answer.

The answer does not always come immediately. A friend, Dr. Bruce Morgan, explained it this way: "We need to be like a cow—take it in and chew on it for a while, like the cow chews the cud before it finally digests the food."

One of the questions I often ask people is: what do you want from God? This would surprise some people, and they didn't really know what they wanted. Some of our prayers and demands to God are so obscure that even He doesn't know what we want.

62

The Better Way

Here are the most frequent questions we were asked during our forty-plus years of ministry:

What is God's will for my life?

What is God saying to me?

Do you have a word for me?

What should I do in this situation?

There were many other questions as well, but most of the questions pertained to hearing God. These folks were all looking for an answer.

Did God hear them and did He answer? I expect He did answer, but perhaps not in the way they expected. I don't believe God wants to keep this knowledge from us. I believe He wants us to know these things, but I think some of these answers are so clear to us that they blind us—so obvious, so simple that we totally overlook them. Of course some answers are not what we want to hear, so we ignore them.

When talking with some of these folks, it became quite clear that the reason they did not understand their answer from God was because they were double-minded. When we are double-minded, no matter how clearly God speaks, we are still confused and unable to make a sound decision. We are afraid we will make a mistake and make the wrong decision.

Some of these folks would try the fleece method. When we are double-minded, that method doesn't work very well either. No matter what sign or wonder takes place, we are still confused.

The difficulty in receiving an answer to many of our questions is because we are dealing with two different realms. One realm is the world kingdom where our natural reasoning and our common sense prevails. This means many of the answers we would get from God would sound like foolishness to us, and we would immediately reject them. The other realm is a spiritual kingdom where the Holy Spirit and our spirit interact.

If I am dealing with the natural realm, then I can look to my own natural reasoning, my common sense and understanding. If I am looking for a spiritual answer, I had better look to my faith, my spirit, and the Holy Spirit—not to my natural reasoning and understanding.

What if I am looking to both of them for the answer? The natural reason is telling me one thing, and my faith is telling me something different. Then we bounce back and forth.

Many times I have asked people if they knew the difference between their soul and spirit. Most of them answered, "I thought they were the same."

> *For the word of God is living and active and sharper than any two-edged sword, and piercing as far as the division of soul and spirit, of both joints and marrow, and able to judge the thoughts and intentions of the heart. (Hebrews 4:12)*

If we don't recognize the difference between our soul and spirit, how do we tell which one is speaking to us?

If we ask the Lord to divide our soul and spirit in such a way that we can tell the difference, He will do it. Then we will be able to tell the difference when our soul is active or our spirit is active. Then we will know what comes from God, and what comes from us. He even shows us what our motives are.

I have heard from the Lord many times, and I have really paid attention when He speaks. It comes as a thought from a different part of my mind than my other thoughts come from. If I do not grab the thought right away and bring it into my memory, it disappears. I know something was there, but it is gone. These God thoughts do not come from the conscious level, they come from the unconscious level, the spiritual level just like the dreams do.

When we pray with our mind or the spoken word, God hears us. What a mind God must have. He hears all of us whether we pray out loud or in the quietness of our mind. We seem to have a problem hearing God, say nothing about hearing one another.

God can speak to us. He has not lost His voice, but there are many other spirits who can speak to us also. These voices can be pretty confusing. Is this voice or thought from God or is it from some other source?

The Bible says to test every spirit. God does not want us to be taken in by every voice or thought we think comes from God. The natural mind can be deceived very easily; our common sense may not be so sensible at all. You cannot trust the natural reasoning if you want to know spiritual truths and answers.

Have you been subtly forced into things you did not want to be involved in?

I expect most of you would have to say, yes! It might have been done through your emotions. Maybe you were made to feel guilty. You were letting people down; people were depending on you. No one else could fill that spot. So you finally gave in, when all the time God was speaking to you through your faith, saying, "No, don't be involved in that!

This happens every day in our homes, our churches, and in our workplaces. It happens to Christians and non-Christians. It can be subtle or sometimes not so subtle control. It is not from God; He does not manipulate or take away our freedom. It is man and other spirits controlling us. There is a better way, a way that is spiritual and free.

63

The Living Word

For the word of God is living and active and sharper than any two-edged sword, and piercing as far as the division of soul and spirit, of both joints and marrow, and able to judge the thoughts and intentions of the heart. And there is no creature hidden from His sight, but all things are open and laid bare to the eyes of Him with whom we have to do.— Hebrews 4:12-13

In Genesis, the first book of the Bible, it says in the very first chapter, verse three: "Then God said." In verse six it says: "Then God said." And again in verse nine: "Then God said." And it continues many more times in the Bible: "Then God said."

This is the living word that Hebrews speaks of, and He has never ceased speaking. Some people hear Him and some do not, because they are either spiritually dead or deaf.

These are the living words that Jesus spoke to the men who were going to stone the woman caught in adultery. He said, "You without sin cast the first stone." These are the seeds Jesus spoke of in the parable of the sower:

The sower went out to sow his seed; and as he sowed, some fell beside the road; and it was trampled underfoot, and the birds of the air ate it up. And other seed fell on rocky soil, and as soon as it grew up, it withered away, because it had no moisture.

And other seed fell among the thorns; and the thorns grew up with it, and choked it out. And other seed fell into the good soil, and grew up, and produced a crop a hundred times as great. And as He said these things, He would call out, "He who has ears to hear, let him hear." (Luke 8:5-8)

Now the parable is this: the seed is *the word of God.* (Luke 8:11)

> *And those beside the road are those who have heard; then the devil comes and takes the word from their heart so that they may not believe and be saved. And those on the rocky soil are those who, when they hear, receive the word with joy; and these have no firm root; they believe for a while, and in time of temptation fall away.*
>
> *And the seeds which fell among the thorns, these are the ones who have heard, and as they go on their way they are choked with worries and riches and pleasures of this life, and bring no fruit to maturity. And the seed in the good soil, these are the ones who have heard the word in an honest and good heart, and hold it fast, and bear fruit with perseverance. (Luke 8:11-15)*

From these Scriptures I have to believe that the living word has fallen on many, many people. The living word comes forth from the Bible. It comes forth through the testimonies of people. It comes forth from churches all around the world. It comes forth through our dreams and visions. The living word comes forth through all the various ministries of the Holy Spirit, and it comes through all the gifts and fruit of the Holy Spirit.

I don't believe any man or woman will be able to stand before God and say, "You didn't send your living word to me!"

All the work and ministry of Jesus was from the living word. Jesus said, "I only do and say what my Father tells me to." If we could only learn to do the same thing! That is God's desire for us, to flow with the living word, day by day in every situation.

This living word has sustained Pauline and Me through all these years of ministry, with strength and healing for us, and healing, miracles, and deliverances for many people wherever we traveled. God has sent the living word to direct us and tell us what to say and do. He wants to do this for all of us if we can only relinquish our control to him, even as Jesus did.

64

Decisions

One area in my Christian walk that I stumbled over many times was making decisions. I was not alone. I found many other Christian people had the same difficulty. *Should I do this? Should I do that?* As a result, we often land up doing nothing.

Many times people have told me they had put out a fleece. I never seemed to get much direction from the fleece. This was the method Gideon used to confirm that he was to go to war.

> *Then Gideon said to God, "If Thou will deliver Israel through me, as Thou has spoken, behold, I will put a fleece of wool on the threshing floor. If there is dew on the fleece only, and it is dry on all the ground, then I will know Thou will deliver Israel through me, as Thou has spoken."*
>
> *And it was so. When he arose early the next morning and squeezed the fleece, he drained the dew from the fleece, a full bowl of water.*
>
> *Then Gideon said to God, "Do not let Thine anger burn against me that I may speak once more; please let me make a test once more with the fleece, let it now be dry only on the fleece, and let there be dew on all the ground." And God did so that night; for it was dry only on the fleece, and dew was on all the ground." (Judges 6:36-40)*

What we have to remember is that God had already told Gideon what he was to do. Gideon was just asking for God to confirm it. Confirmation is something God gives us after the fact. Signs and miracles will often happen after God's message is delivered to an individual or a group, to confirm the message was from God.

We want God to make our decisions, and He will not! We then use the fleece method, trying to force God to make our decision. The fleece method is very iffy. In most decisions we don't need a fleece; what we need to do is make a firm decision. Then God can show us in many ways whether we have made the right decision.

How can God show you if you have made a right or wrong decision until after you have made it? You must also remember we are not Old Testament people like Gideon was; we are New Testament people, and the living Word is written in our hearts. We have the Holy Spirit to guide and direct each one of us.

We ask the Lord, "What do you want me to do?"

His reply: "I've been showing you for months and you are not paying attention. You are thinking maybe you should do this, maybe you should do that, and you do nothing. I give you a dream. I have someone suggest something, and you pay no attention. I give you a message in church, I point you to a Scripture, but you take nothing personal. How can I speak to you?"

When God wants us to do something special, as in the case with Gideon, He can make it very clear. At this point our faith is involved. Was that really God speaking to me? I personally believe we can come to the place where we recognize God's voice as soon as He speaks to us, the same as knowing my wife's voice or my father's voice. The New Testament is about a personal walking and talking relationship with God.

Gideon did not have to make a decision until after God spoke to him. There are many decisions we make every day apart from God that are a part of our daily life. Most of these decisions are not important decisions, just necessary ones.

When God speaks and gives us direction or warning, we need to pay attention. When we are about to speak or do something, and the Lord says: "Don't say that or do that," we would be wise not to do it.

We as Christian people are called to be servants, priests and ministers. When God is speaking to us as priests and servants, He is telling us what to do, where to go, what to say. Now we have to make a decision: am I going to do it, or do I tell Him I don't want to do it? Do I argue with Him, or do I make a decision on the spot and say, "Yes, Lord, just tell me what to say and show me how to accomplish this."

When the Lord gives you a specific thing to do, He gives you everything you need to accomplish it. God gave Gideon everything he needed to fight a war and win.

A friend was going on a trip and decided to leave on a particular day. He said the Lord told him to leave a day later. He looked at the weather report and there were going to be storms on the way if he waited another day. He made a decision based on the weather report instead of by faith in what the Lord told him.

If the Lord made it clear to wait a day longer, He was ready to do something; some circumstances somewhere along the way could even have been to save their lives.

When therefore he heard that he was sick, He stayed then two days longer in the place where He was. (John 11:6)

The Lord is not worried about the weather. He wants us to apply faith and trust Him and be in certain places at certain times. We don't have any difficulty making decisions when the desire of the flesh and emotions are involved—only when faith is involved.

When it is time to make decisions, whether God has spoken to us or not, it is good to speak to Him. First, ask Him for wisdom and knowledge to make a good decision. Then, when you have decided what your decision is, tell Him exactly what it is you are going to do. If the Lord would have you do things in a different way, He can tell you. If you are making a mistake, He can tell you.

But note whether you have peace in your heart and spirit; if you do, you are right on. The Lord gives us a lamp to our feet—He does not want us walking in darkness.

65

St. Paul – Apostle & Teacher

And when I came to you, brethren, I did not come with superiority of speech or of wisdom, proclaiming to you the testimony of God. For I determined to know nothing among you except Jesus Christ, and Him crucified. And I was with you in weakness and in fear and in much trembling.

And my message and my preaching were not in persuasive words of wisdom, but in demonstration of the Spirit and of power, that you faith should not rest on the wisdom of men, but on the power of God—1 Corinthians 2:1-5.

St. Paul's teaching in the Bible has had a greater impact on my life than any other part of the Bible. It was Paul's letters that taught me to function as a spiritual man. Through his teaching I learned to know the difference between the "letter of the law that kills" and "the Spirit of the law that brings life."

All the other apostles walked with Jesus while He was still on the earth. Paul was not even called to be an apostle until after Jesus was raised from the dead. When Paul experienced the Lord Jesus, He had already been glorified and was the King of Kings; He had already risen from the grave and returned to heaven.

Why was St. Paul called to be such a teacher?

He was already a teacher, one of the great teachers in Israel! Paul knew the law, but after he had a conversion experience, he understood how deadly the law was and that he was responsible for having people killed, thinking he was doing God a favor.

This is still happening in the religions of the world today. People are being killed, and the ones doing it think they are obeying God.

Paul was a very dedicated, committed man of God before his conversion, but after his conversion, he was maybe more committed than he had been before.

And when I came to you, brethren, I did not come with superiority of speech or of wisdom, proclaiming to you the testimony of God. (I Corinthians 2:1)

St. Paul had the ability to come with wisdom and superior speech, but he knew that would not change anyone. The law does not have the power to change people.

For I determined to know nothing among you except Jesus Christ, and Him crucified. (1 Corinthians 2:2)

Why did St. Paul put so much emphasis on Jesus Christ and Him crucified? He knew that is where the life is; Jesus is the only answer. That is where all the power is to change us. There is no other way, no other hope for any of us.

And I was with you in weakness and in fear and in much trembling. (I Corinthians 2:3)

St. Paul was aware that he could do nothing to change anybody; He was weak and fearful, and it did not even matter.

And my message and my preaching were not in persuasive words of wisdom of wisdom, but in demonstration of the Spirit and of power, ... (1Corinthians 2:4)

St. Paul was not trying to persuade anybody, anywhere. He could have used those abilities because he had them. But he choose to let the Holy Spirit have His way so that the *living word* touched their lives with power to heal and change them.

that your faith should not rest on the wisdom of men, but on the power of God. (1 Corinthians 2:5)

This now leaves us with the question: does your faith rest on the wisdom of men or on the power of God?

For many years my faith rested on the wisdom of men—even as my life was falling apart. In desperation I cried out to God. He heard me and the Holy Spirit touched my life with the power of God. Now my faith rests on God's power touching my life, instead of the wisdom of men.

Through St. Paul, I came to understand and realize the difference between the Old Testament and the New Testament. Many church people today are still functioning under the Old Testament and don't even realize it. Some of these people are church leaders, but because they do not know how to be led by the Holy Spirit, they are unable to teach others.

St. Paul made it very clear that the New Covenant is God's Word written in our hearts. The Old Covenant was written in tablets of stone, and no matter how hard we try to obey them we will fail. The living word is written in our hearts, and if we desire to, we can obey it.

> *... you are a letter of Christ, cared for by us, written not with ink, but with the Spirit of the living God, not on tablets of stone, but on tablets of human hearts ... who also made us adequate as servants of a new covenant, not of the letter, but of the Spirit ...* (2 Corinthians 3:3-6)

66

The Holy Spirit

The Holy Spirit is like the wind; you can see His effects, you can sense Him moving, but you cannot control Him. There are many spirits in the world, but He is the greatest. He is aware of everything that is happening. The Holy Spirit can be like a mighty storm affecting many lives, or He can be so still that you are not even aware of Him. God is the Holy Spirit and the Holy Spirit is God. He is to be esteemed, honored, and respected.

Jesus Christ is the only way into the kingdom of God. The Holy Spirit is the one who will guide you there. The Holy Spirit is filled with light and life; He leads us out of the darkness into the light. Without Him we would never escape the darkness, and we would never be empowered to overcome Satan.

Jesus Christ hung on the cross and His last words were: "*It is finished!" And He bowed His head, and gave up His spirit.* (John 19:30).

What does this mean? It means that the work of Jesus was finished. He had accomplished the work His Father had sent Him to do. Days later He ascended into heaven and was seated at the right hand of God. Jesus prepared the way so the Holy Spirit could come and accomplish His work in each one of us. The Father is also seated in heaven, but it is the Holy Spirit who is on this earth to accomplish the will of the Father.

The Holy Spirit is everywhere on this earth. He is involved with nations and is aware of all the activity going on in the world. He is involved with the choice of leaders and lifting them up and bringing them down. He is aware of the groaning of the earth and the people on it. For the most part, these leaders and powers have very little awareness of the Holy Spirit

Sometimes He chooses to reveal Himself; sometimes He

chooses to remain hidden. We cannot tell Him what to do. He accomplishes the will of the Father. He is like the wind, the air we breathe; He surrounds the earth. This wind can knock us down or it can lift us up.

As Christian people, we can grieve the Holy Spirit. Paul said:

And do not grieve the Holy Spirit of God, by whom you were sealed for the day of redemption (Ephesians 4:30).

Many times in our ignorance and childishness we say and do things that would grieve the Holy Spirit of God. Thank God, He is not easily grieved.

This is what it says in Isaiah 63:10:

But they rebelled and grieved His Holy Spirit; Therefore, He turned Himself to become their enemy, He fought against them.

I believe King Saul is an example of someone grieving the Spirit of God.

The Holy Spirit is the most powerful Person on this earth. If the Holy Spirit and the Spirit- filled church were removed from the earth, Satan would have free reign. At some point in the future Satan is going to have free reign on this earth, for a period of time. God help you if you have not turned to the Lord. When Jesus takes His church, the hindrance will be removed and Satan will have free reign.

In Him, you also, after listening to the message of truth, the gospel of your salvation—having also believed, you were sealed in Him with the Holy Spirit of promise, who is given as a pledge of our inheritance, with a view to the redemption of God's own possession, to the praise of His glory. (Ephesians 1:13-14)

The Holy Spirit does not reveal Himself to the world—only to God's people. He is a seal from God to us, proclaiming, "These are My people." It is an assurance from God, saying, "I acknowledge you as mine."

Some people are much more aware of this seal of the Holy Spirit than others. A person who is real sensitive to the Holy Spirit can recognize others who are sealed by the Holy Spirit.

Some people have been sealed by the Holy Spirit for years and are not aware of it. There are others who have been told they have been sealed by the Holy Spirit, but are not. They have been deceived by the religion of man.

It is truly amazing: the Person of the Holy Spirit is the greatest power on this earth, yet few people know Him. He does wonderful miracles and healings, but only a few of the people who receive these gifts seem to be aware of it.

The Holy Spirit touches thousands of lives every day as His Spirit soars round the earth, accomplishing God's will. God has given two of the most valuable gifts that anyone could ever hope to receive: His Son, Jesus Christ, and the Holy Spirit.

Here is another special work the Holy Spirit does for us:

> *"When the Helper comes, whom I will send to you from the Father, that is the Spirit of truth, who proceeds from the Father, He will bear witness of Me, and you will bear witness also, because you have been with Me from the beginning." (John 15:26-27)*

The Holy Spirit witnesses directly to our spirit the truth of Jesus Christ. Because we now have the truth, and we know it is the truth, we can witness to the world that Jesus Christ is the Son of God and was the lamb sacrificed for our sins.

67

The Opposition

For all who are being led by the Holy Spirit, these are the sons of God.—Romans 8:14

Why is it important that we be led by the Spirit? I think the following Scripture answers that question very well:

But I say, walk by the Spirit, and you will not carry out the desire of the flesh. For the flesh sets its desire against the Spirit, and the Spirit against the flesh; for these are in opposition to one another, so that you may not do the things you please. But if you are led by the Spirit, you are not under the Law. (Galatians 5:16-18)

We have many things to contend with in this world. Some of them are natural and some are spiritual. How well we handle these contentious things is very important.

Some of us simply try to ignore these things and hope they will go away; they don't! There are worldly cares around us that must be dealt with. As Christian people we also have Satan and the evil spirits to contend with. We also have another enemy in our spiritual journey: our very own flesh. I sometimes think this is our biggest enemy of all.

If we get our attention fixed on Satan and the evil spirits and ignore our very own flesh, we land up defeated time and again. It seems to take us a long time to realize just how strong our fleshly desires are. It is these strong desires in our flesh that our enemy Satan takes advantage of.

I find then the principle that evil is present in me, the one who wishes to do good. (Romans 7:21)

How many of us really want to believe there is evil in us? Most of us probably don't want to believe it. If Satan can convince us that there is no evil in us, then we believe the lie instead of the truth. If we cannot recognize there is evil in us, how are we going to defeat it?

Where did this evil come from, and how did it become a part of us?

It came from the Garden of Eden, from the tree of good and evil. When Adam and Eve ate from the tree of the knowledge of good and evil, the evil became a part of them. As their descendants, it has passed down to every one of us in our flesh.

Flesh and blood cannot inherit the Kingdom of God! Why? Because it is contaminated with evil. Our soul can be restored and our spirit can be born again, but there is no hope for our flesh; it has to die. Evil is condemned to this earth, just as surely as Satan is, and cannot leave it.

> *And the Lord God commanded the man, saying, 'From any tree of the garden you may eat freely; but from the tree of the knowledge of good and evil you shall not eat, for in the day that you eat from it you shall surely die.' (Genesis 2:16-17)*

If we have the Holy Spirit and know how to use the authority God has given us, we can defeat Satan and the evil spirits. But defeating the desires of the flesh is altogether different.

This is not a battle where you fight hard get the victory and it is over. This is a battle where it is only by the power of the Holy Spirit, and our own spirit developing and becoming stronger, that we can overcome the desires of the flesh.

If you have had children, you must have seen how quickly they become strong-minded at a very early age. They also can become very stubborn, wanting to have control of their world. This is soul power.

Soul power is much stronger in some folks than it is in others. If you have strong soul power, it can really resist the Holy Spirit and keep your spirit from rising to its proper level. Our spirit should have the highest position in our being, with our soul and body below, in that order.

Our spirit, with the help of the Holy Spirit, can develop and become strong enough to take control away from our soul and our body. Then evil in us can be defeated, day after day.

The problems that some of our well-known pastors, ministers, and priests have fallen into is a result of evil in their flesh. Do you think these people wanted to become involved in these things? I don't think so! The spirit in them was not mature enough, nor was it strong enough, to overcome the desires of their flesh or their soul.

Some people think that if their conscience does not bother them or convict them, they are okay. Our conscience is a part of our fallen nature; it is sick and weak just as much as the rest of our fallen nature. It is only through our spiritual man that we can begin to really see sin for what it is.

We cannot trust our body and we cannot trust our soul; they will lie to us and deceive us.

> *But a natural man does not accept the things of the Spirit of God; for they are foolishness to him, and he cannot understand them for they are spiritually appraised. But he who is spiritual appraises all things, yet he himself is appraised by no man. (1 Corinthians 2:14-15)*

68

Full Assurance

Assurance: we talk about it and we sing about it, but do we have it? What are we to have assurance in? It is interesting that the word "assurance" sounds so much like the word "insurance." Maybe assurance is a lot like insurance.

Insurance is for our future needs—if our house burns down, if we have a car accident, or for natural things we many need in the future. *Assurance* is also for our future, our spiritual future.

Assurance is an interesting word. My dictionary describes it this way: 1) The act of assuring or the state of being assured. 2) A statement or indication that inspires confidence; a guarantee. 3) Freedom from doubt.

Some people carry more *insurance* than they need, because they worry about their future here on earth. Yet they do not give a second thought to their future, to when they will leave this earth. This Scripture tells us there is a lot of wealth that comes with being fully assured; this wealth is a true knowledge of Christ Himself.

> *... that their hearts may be encouraged, having been knit together in love, and attaining to all the wealth that comes from the full assurance of understanding, resulting in a true knowledge of God's mystery, that is, Christ Himself. (Colossians 2:2)*

Now we can understand why St. Paul, in spite of his knowledge of the Law, was so determined to know nothing but Christ Himself.

The following Scripture gives us the clearest picture of what faith is. Faith is conviction and assurance combined together. Faith give us something that is immovable, something that is rock solid.

68 Full Assurance

Now faith is the assurance of things hoped for, the conviction of things not seen. (Hebrews 11:1)

There is a difference between hope and faith. The difference is that hope is not yet convinced, the assurance has not yet formed in the heart and spirit. We are *almost* convinced, but not quite. When the assurance and the conviction join, we have faith.

Just as an example, I am convinced in my heart and spirit that there is life after death. I am fully convinced that Jesus Christ died on the cross for my sins. I have full assurance in my heart that Jesus Christ is the son of God.

And we desire that each one of you show the same diligence so as to realize the full assurance of hope until the end. (Hebrews 6:11)

We can have assurance, but not be fully assured. What we need is full assurance. This comes with the true knowledge of God's mystery, Christ Himself. This is talking about revelation in our heart; it involves a personal relationship with Jesus Christ. When this personal relationship happens between an individual and Jesus, a full assurance and confidence comes with it.

We can go to the right church, know the Bible from end to end, go to an altar call time and again, yet still not have a full assurance in our heart, a true relationship with Jesus. This is so important. This was the same problem that Jesus spoke of:

"You search the Scriptures, because you think that in them you have eternal life; and it is these that bear witness of Me; and you are unwilling to come to Me, that you may have life." (John 5:39-40.

It has always been our thinking that has created a problem with our relationship with God. Now it creates a problem in our relationship with Jesus Christ too. Our thinking undermines our assurance and confidence and, as a result, our faith.

... let us draw near with a sincere heart in full assurance of faith, having our hearts sprinkled clean from an evil conscience and our bodies washed with pure water (Hebrews 10:22).

69

A Place of Rest

Peace and rest go hand in hand. We will never find *rest* until we find peace. We can spend a lifetime struggling with one thing or another. Some of the things we struggle with are very important, while others really have no importance at all.

I recall Pauline sharing how she thought that when she got married, she would find what was missing in her life. But she found out that she was still dissatisfied. Then she thought when she had children, she would be satisfied. After she had three children, she found she was still lacking something.

We all have a void in our life that nothing seems to fill. People struggle for many years to reach a place that seems unreachable. Some become very wealthy and others struggle to be the best in their field of expertise. Others become great movie stars or sport figures. Many of them on the way destroy themselves.

What is it we are trying to find that keeps us unsettled for so many years of our lives? What is it that drives us to these heights? We try everything the world has to offer, and find it is still not enough.

I think of the parable of the Prodigal Son. Both sons were unhappy; one stayed home, the other left. It was the one who left that finally found peace and rest.

It is something within us that was lost when man fell from God's grace. It seems there is a cry from the very depths of our souls: "How long, O' Lord, before we can find a place of rest and peace for our souls?" I think all of us touch upon it once in a while, but it is very elusive, here for a moment and then gone again.

Sometimes we want to hide from the world, because when we look at the world very closely, whatever measure of peace and joy we have achieved is gone. I think even the earth is waiting to find peace and rest.

Strange as it seems, the *rest* is not far from us—no farther than the kingdom of God in us, yet it sometimes seems so hard to find. Some people find the place of rest. We know this because we can see they are resting in the midst of confusion and business.

No one else can find the place of rest for us. Others can point the way for us, but we must find it. Whether we are the prodigal son or the one who stays home, we can only find it where we are.

In order to find this rest, we must find who we are and stop mimicking others. We are hidden in Christ. When we find Him, then we find who and what we are.

There are people who believe in God and have accepted Him as Savior who are still fighting with God. These people will not find rest until they stop fighting with God and accept themselves—as imperfect as they might be.

70

A More Excellent Way

But earnestly desire the greater gifts. And I show you a more excellent way.—1 Corinthians 12:31

The gifts of the Holy Spirit are wonderful. The world needs them, the church needs them, and we need them. But there is a lot of ignorance about the gifts of the Holy Spirit. We are more apt to argue over them or write books about them than we are to use them.

What is the more excellent way that St. Paul is speaking about? I have come to discover through many years of ministry that the more excellent way is the fruit of the Spirit, not the gifts of the Spirit. We need the gifts of the Spirit, because we lack the fruit of the Spirit.

Many years ago, at the beginning of our ministry, God blessed me with the peace that passes understanding. I did not realize for several years what a wonderful blessing it was. As time went on, I found I could pass this peace from God on to others.

A few years later I received the joy of the Lord. I discovered I could also pass this joy on to others. As God's love became more established in my heart and spirit, I found I could also pass that on to others.

Faith also became much more active in my life, and I began to see faith had a very clear voice from God that could light the path before me. What I came to see was that the fruit of the Spirit is greater in bringing healing to others than are the gifts of the Holy Spirit.

As the years went by, I relied more and more on giving away the fruit of the Spirit to people who were in need. We would bring them peace, joy, faith and love; and people would receive healing—in their physical bodies, in their emotions, in their minds, and in their spirits. There is tremendous healing power in every one of the fruits of the Holy Spirit.

You cannot give away something you do not have. I often have heard people speak on peace, joy and love. There were some wonderful messages and preaching, but the lives of some of these folks did not seem to have much peace, joy or love in them. As a result, there was no healing that took place, unless the gifts of the Holy Spirit would be manifested.

What I did see over many years was the difference between the fruit of the Spirit and the gifts of the Spirit. I saw that the fruit brought a deeper and longer lasting healing to people than the gifts did. The signs and wonders of the miracle-healing gifts and the words of wisdom and knowledge would be quickly forgotten by those who received them, sometimes almost immediately, other times in a matter of days.

If we want to bring healing to others, we must be in touch with the river of living water that flows out of our innermost being. We must be in touch with the kingdom of God within us. Once we have received these wonderful fruits we can freely give them away.

We can speak words of peace, joy and love, or we can just touch people and release peace, love and joy to them. I have done this many times. It is a wonderful experience because we can feel these things as they are happening. We can cause faith and hope to rise up in people who have none. We can do all the things that Jesus did.

About the Author

Born in Lyndonville, VT, the youngest of five children, Ralph Nault was raised Roman Catholic. After serving as a Marine in the Korean War, Ralph and his young wife, Pauline, settled into Vermont's Northeast Kingdom. Ralph drove a tractor-trailer truck for years, then became an electrical contractor.

At age 32, he was miserable, discouraged, headed for divorce, and suicidal. When Ralph fell prone on the floor at the church altar and cried out for help, the Lord responded and transformed his life and marriage. He accepted the vision God gave him to become a "water boy," giving a spiritual drink of living water to anyone who needed it.

Thousands of people have had their spiritual thirst slaked as Ralph and Pauline have traveled around the country, sharing their testimonies and delivering a word of life in home meetings, churches, and other venues. The effectiveness of their ministry comes from the power of the Holy Spirit working through them. Their work is marked by numerous physical and emotional healings, and by seeing people set free from bondages and their lives restored.

One day in another dramatic visionary encounter, the Lord removed the water boy image and told Ralph that he was now a "spiritual father." Since then Ralph and Pauline have functioned as spiritual parents, mentoring and encouraging others.

Author of several other books on Christian spirituality, Ralph writes a blog (http://www.ralphnault.com/blog/), email newsletters and social media postings that are a blessing to many people hungry for more in their walk with God.

http://www.ralphnault.com